Cooking &
Entertaining
on Your
Boat

The Editors of Chapman Piloting
and
Elizabeth Wheeler

A Chapman Nautical Guide

Hearst Books
A Division of Sterling Publishing Co., Inc.
New York

Produced by Bill Smith Studio

Recipes developed by: Hope Farrell, Sandra Rose Gluck, Ann Hardy Pettingill, Roberta Rall, and Sallie Y. Williams

Library of Congress Cataloging-in-Publication Data
Cooking and entertaining on your boat / by the editors of Chapman.
p. cm. – (A Chapman nautical guide)
ISBN 1-58816-084-X
1. Cookery, Marine. 2. Entertaining. I. Series

TX840.M7 C66 2002
641.5'753—dc21   2001039862

10 9 8 7 6 5 4 3 2 1

Published by Hearst Books
A Division of Sterling Publishing Co., Inc.
387 Park Avenue South, New York, N.Y. 10016

CHAPMAN and CHAPMAN PILOTING and Hearst Books are trademarks
owned by Hearst Communications, Inc.

Distributed in Canada by Sterling Publishing
c/o Canadian Manda Group, One Atlantic Avenue, Suite 105
Toronto, Ontario, Canada M6K 3E7

Distributed in Australia by Capricorn Link (Australia) Pty. Ltd.
P.O. Box 704, Windsor, NSW 2756 Australia
Printed in China

ISBN 1-58816-084-X

TABLE OF CONTENTS

Stocking Up

The water is smooth and calm as you ghost into the cove and set anchor. Everyone is sun-kissed, relaxed, and tired. The kids are playing peacefully. Soon, as the sun gets lower, stomachs start to growl. It's time for dinner. Being on the water has a way of whipping up appetites.

Good food and plenty of it make for a successful and pleasurable cruise. Even if you've never cooked on board, you'll find it easy to satisfy those hungry sailors if you remember one thing—don't try to cook the way you would at home. Whether your cooking facilities are as primitive as a one-burner stove, a bowl, and a jug of water, or a fully equipped modern galley, there are some basic frustrations to cooking on a boat. You'll find yourself chasing an onion as the boat rocks, and you'll quickly discover that ice-cream isn't a great seagoing dessert. But that won't stop you from serving up crew-pleasers such as Homestyle Chicken Stew and Cincinnati Chili. The secret is to use common sense, keep it simple, and follow the motto of sailors and scouts alike: "Be prepared." You can whip up memorable meals and still have plenty of time to enjoy yourself along the way.

This recipe collection gives you smart strategies for overcoming the limitations of a seagoing kitchen and keeping the crew happy. You'll find recipes that you can prepare at home, then reheat on board. You'll also discover simple dishes featuring fresh ingredients that are easy to prepare in the confines of a boat. Finally, there are great meal ideas that rely on packaged ingredients—perfect for long cruises when fresh supplies are harder to find.

WHAT'S YOUR STYLE?

Traveling on a boat is an adventure—a departure from the normal comforts of home—and that's part of the fun. It is reasonable to expect that meals aboard will be different from your accustomed fare. Honestly assess the amount of time and energy you are willing to invest in keeping your crew well fed; stick to it, and everyone will be happy.

Before stocking your boat for a trip, consider your own preferences, the people you'll feed, your equipment, and the weather—all will influence how you approach the task of providing meals. Do you enjoy planning and preparing feasts, or would you be happy with soup and sandwiches? Are you a lone cook who wants to do it all, or are you comfortable assigning cooking tasks to your crew?

Even with the quickened appetites that fresh air produces, people will be happy with simple fare, as long as it's plentiful and delicious. Your crew may be content with sandwiches and chips or grilled burgers with deli potato salad. But more elaborate fare need not be a drain on the cook. By mixing store-bought items with homemade, you won't need to prepare all the fixings for every meal. And, if you bring on board some dishes you prepared at home and supplement with a few simple recipes to make underway, you can ensure mouth-watering meals throughout your cruise. Even non-gourmets on your crew will appreciate the effort.

GETTING STARTED

Three major factors will influence your menu plans:

1. Cooking facilities

A galley that boasts a freezer, refrigerator, microwave, and a full-sized stove and cook top means you can plan more ambitious menus than you would for a boat equipped with a single burner and an ice chest. Either way, relax! Even with minimal equipment, you will be able to provide tasty, satisfying meals on board.

2. Itinerary

If you are going port to port, you can count on a decent amount of time and calm to prepare meals while docked. On the other hand, if you know you will be beating upwind in a choppy sea, it makes sense to prepare one-dish meals than you can simply heat and serve, or cold sandwiches and cookies. And consider the weather. A sultry summer cruise suggests cold meals and grilling menus, while a fall frostbiter trip calls for hot meals with plenty of calories.

3. Your audience

Needs and appetites vary. A boat full of brawny, active, twenty-somethings will pack away an astonishing amount of food, while young children, neophyte sailors, and older folks may eat less, or have their own particular needs. If you are traveling with non-family members, survey them in advance about their food likes and dislikes. You should also check out your crew members' level of boating experience. Sailing newcomers may stop eating the first day or so out. However, most regain normal eating habits in a day or two, while some who are accustomed to particular schedules and cues in their environments adjust more slowly or not at all. Some may develop an aversion toward food. Those who lose their appetites should be monitored to make sure they're not succumbing to seasickness or dehydration. Sometimes, out of anxiety or boredom, a person will swing the other way and will develop a ravenous appetite. The only problem with big eaters is that you may lose your ship's stores too quickly. Be sure to provide plentiful snacks and keep them in a clearly marked locker. A bountiful snack locker will keep your crew from raiding the icebox and devouring the food you planned to serve for dinner.

FEEDING THE SENSITIVE, SEASICK AND HOMESICK

Here are a few tips that will help you keep all of the sailors well fed and content:

- Get a good head start. Prepare all the snacks and meals you'll need for the first day out at home before embarking. When stomachs rumble, you'll be able to get meals ready quickly while you get used to the new galley routine.

- To help control queasiness, make sure everyone has eaten before you get underway, but have them stay away from greasy, spicy foods.

- Make sure that meals and snacks eaten underway are easy to handle. Serve finger foods such as sandwiches, fruit, granola bars, chunks of cheese, and boneless oven-fried chicken.

- Be sure to bring along favorite snacks and cookies and plan a few "comfort food" meals that you know your family or guests will enjoy. A favorite food will do wonders for a person who is feeling blue or out of sorts, as will the knowledge that someone cares enough to bring it just for them.

- Bring along ready-to-eat foods that are easy on the stomach such as plain crackers, rice crackers, melba toast, and other bland foods such as bananas.

- Repackage cereals, crackers, and crunchy snacks into smaller, airtight containers to keep them crisp. No one likes these foods when they get soggy or stale.

- Make sure everyone has enough to drink on hot days. Give kids their own personal drinking cups. They'll love drinking from them, and it will be easy to keep them refilled with bottled beverages or your own homemade drink mixes.

- Keep an eye on the adults, too. Sometimes people will avoid drinking fluids so they won't have to go below to use the head, which can lead to dehydration. If they are listless or feel cold on a hot day, suggest sipping water.

- Encourage anyone who is feeling queasy to sip plain water, ginger ale, or bouillon. She or he may feel too ill to drink, but it's important that the person doesn't get dehydrated. Offer plain crackers or bread at mealtimes.

- Get the seasick on deck in the fresh air where they can see the horizon, and treat them with compassion.

- Go light on the alcohol in mixed drinks or serve non-alcoholic drinks. Being out on the water in the sun and wind all day can be dehydrating—and so are alcoholic drinks. The combination can be a double whammy.

- Buy boxed, shelf-stable milk such as Long-life or Parmalat if you have limited refrigeration and for emergencies in case you run out of fresh milk.

KNOW YOUR EQUIPMENT

Imagine discovering on your first day out that the pan of lasagne that you are about to put into the oven doesn't fit. Fortunately, it's in a disposable foil pan, so you scrunch up the edges and shove it in, but half an hour later a sizzling sound and a burning smell tell you that the pan cracked when you bent it and now sauce is running all over the bottom of the oven. Worse yet, you have six more casseroles in the same size pan waiting in the bottom of the icebox. Fortunately, this doesn't have to happen: Check the size of your galley stove before you leave. They differ from one boat to the next, but most are smaller than a home stove. The simple solution is to use smaller pans.

Prior to the start of a cruise, it's wise to familiarize yourself with all the galley's equipment. You want to make sure all the parts are there and that everything is in good working order. Do the stove and refrigerator run on electric power or gas? If you need electricity to run the stove and refrigerator, it makes sense to plan to do your cooking at a marina. That way, you'll avoid running the boat's noisy generator more than necessary.

GALLEY BASICS: FIRE, WATER, AND ICE

FIRE

Most boat stoves are smaller versions of home stoves, usually with two or more burners and an oven. However, they are a little harder to use, especially if they are alcohol-powered. So it's smart to plan on preparing recipes that don't require precision baking or steady, high-powered burners. While alcohol is inexpensive, it delivers the least

THE STOVE:

✓ Gas, alcohol or
electric?

✓ If it's gas, is
it propane,
natural gas
or butane?

✓ What are the
oven's internal
dimensions?

✓ Will it hold an
entire long loaf
of garlic bread
or will you have
to cut the loaf
in half?

WATER:

✓ How much fresh
water does your
boat's tank
hold?

✓ Is it potable?

✓ Do you have a
salt-water pump
in the galley?

ICE:

✓ Are you using
coolers or an
icebox with
blocks of ice?

✓ Or do you have
a refrigerator
and freezer unit
that must run
off the engine?

intense heat and can be agonizingly slow. People who cook prefer propane because it delivers the fastest, hottest flame. Compressed natural gas ("CNG") works well, but delivers far less heat per unit of fuel than propane, which means you'll have to carry larger tanks or refill more frequently. More importantly, CNG is readily available only on the West Coast.

If you plan to bake or roast, you'll want a gas- or an electric-powered stove, with gas performing better. Get an oven thermometer to help monitor the temperature. Most powerboats over 35 feet are equipped with electric stoves, usually with flat cast-iron burners mounted on ceramic tops or ceramic smooth-top units with electric elements mounted underneath the surface. The stove top provides additional counter space when not in use.

Many sailboat stoves are gimbaled—set on a pivot that allows them to swing with the boat's movement. When not in use, they are latched to hold them in place. The cook tops are fitted with "fiddles," special adjustable clamps that hold pots securely on the stove while the boat is moving. Gimbaled stoves are especially important for sailors who will be cooking underway on long trips.

Portable one-burner stoves fueled with butane canisters produce a very hot flame and are convenient for cooking if you are at a calm anchorage or dock. They can be used just about anywhere if set on a flat surface and sheltered from wind. Fuel canisters last about 45 minutes each, so it is wise to keep a supply on hand.

For important information on safe use of boat stoves, see Chapter 2.

WATER

When you are accustomed to having clean water for washing and drinking with the turn of a faucet, it is easy to take water for granted. But on a cruise, you will be limited to the fresh water you can carry in the boat's tanks and in water jugs. While you probably can drink the water from your storage tanks, you may find it has an off taste, even with the most careful cleaning and filtering. You are better off lugging bottled water on board for drinking and cooking and using the boat's water for rinsing. As a rule of thumb, figure two gallons of fresh water per person per day for all drinking, cooking, tooth-brushing, and washing. Store plastic water jugs upright in the bilge or in lockers that drain in case they leak.

COLD STORAGE

Refrigeration on a boat is a wonderful amenity that will allow you to store a wide range of foods as well as the all-important cold drinks. But it does require a little vigilance to keep the flow of food and drink cool and safe. A large powerboat can support a full-size refrigerator, but most boats have two lesser options available:

• One is an insulated box outfitted with an electric cooling unit much like your home refrigerator that circulates a coolant through coils to draw heat away. You can use this pretty much as you would your home refrigerator.

• The other is an insulated icebox that holds block ice. Most are deep, top-loading models that require long arms to reach the bottom. Side-opening models are available, but top-loading models tend to stay cold longer because cold air sinks. Side-opening models are a little more convenient for rummaging around, and in fact invite that behavior, but whenever the door is opened, cold air escapes.

Aside from keeping the lid closed, the quality of the insulation around the box is key to maintaining temperatures at the safest level. (See Chapter 2 for more information on food storage.) You can bring along portable iceboxes, but they are best used for limited cold storage and for keeping drinks and food cold for a short time.

COOLERS

They are among the most important pieces of equipment you will use for your cruise. Coolers are essential for keeping frozen and refrigerated foods cold when you transport them from the supermarket and for keeping

SALTWATER RINSE

Rinse your dirty dishes clean with salt water. For best results, use fresh water for the final wash and rinse.

drinks cold while you are sailing. Rigid coolers take up space. The soft, canvas covered cooler bags offer more options. They fold down nicely for storage and can even be used to carry clothes. They retain the cold as well as other coolers and won't scratch surfaces or bark shins. Whichever model you choose, use ice packs to help keep the temperature down during transport. The rigid permanent ice packs last indefinitely, while the soft plastic pillow-type ice packs eventually break and leak a sticky gel.

COOKING TOOLS

To prepare wonderful meals on a boat, you need only the most basic tools and equipment. To save valuable galley space, choose items that can do more than one job. For example, you can use a set of stainless-steel nesting mixing bowls with flat, snap-on plastic lids for mixing, serving, and storing food. They can take heat or double as a gelatin mold. Plastic is unbreakable, light, and generally inexpensive. Its only faults are that it will gouge and melt easily and will develop a greasy patina that requires plenty of soap and hot water to remove.

KNIVES

The most important kitchen tools are good sharp knives. Second-rate knives from the back of the kitchen drawer will not do for the boat. A dull, chipped knife is not only frustrating to use, it is a real hazard because it requires extra force to chop and slice. And the risk of slipping and giving yourself a bad cut increases in tight quarters on a moving boat.

An all-purpose chef's knife and several paring knives will take care of most cutting and chopping chores. A well-made serrated knife is a bonus. Look for good-quality knives made of vanadium steel (one brand is "Global"), which sharpens well. (German stainless-steel knives do not take an edge easily.) Vanadium will discolor some, especially in corrosive salt air, so dry knives well after washing. Never leave a good knife jammed into a wet pile of cutlery—it's dangerous, will ruin the edge, and corrode the metal. Slip blades into knife guards when you put them away (see sidebar).

A word of caution: Your nice knives will be very attractive to a crew member who needs to cut a piece of line or chop through a cardboard box. Make it plain that your galley knives are to be used only for food preparation and are not fair game. Stock up on a few box-cutters with replaceable blades to have ready when you hear the inevitable cry for "something sharp, right NOW!"

Even if you are careful about storing knives and manage to keep them away from deck hands, they will still require occasional sharpening. If you do not have the patience or skill to use a sharpening stone, take your knives to a sharpening service, or run them through a knife sharpening device. A good sharpening steel will go a long way towards keeping your knives honed, but eventually they will have to have their edges reset.

POTS AND PANS

On a boat, you want heavy pots and pans that will stay put on the stove, won't warp, and can take getting knocked around without getting dented. The heavy-duty professional-quality lines sold at better kitchenware stores are perfect. If you want to save money, try shopping for good used heavy-weight pots and pans at garage sales or at a restaurant supply house.

Make sure you have one (or ideally two) three- to four-quart heavy enameled cast-iron pot with a lid. It is big enough to hold a stew and potatoes for six hungry people. These pots often pop up at tag sales, usually with a little chip missing on the edge. While imperfect, they are still serviceable and will practically last forever.

A good nonstick frying pan is great for pancakes, omelets, and fritattas. To protect the surface, use a plastic spatula and never scrub the pan with a scouring pad. Rinse it out and wipe it dry after each use. Another multi-use pot is a large (10- to 12-quart) kettle made from

KNIFE GUARDS

Usually when you purchase a good knife, it comes with its own cardboard or plastic case, which makes a great guard. If you don't have one, make one with a piece of cardboard, such as the cardboard backing from a pad of paper, and duct tape.

enameled metal, such as graniteware available in hardware stores. It is useful for making or heating soup, steaming vegetables, cooking pasta or clams, or even icing down drinks if you've run out of cooler space. It can also be put on top of a grill to cook lobsters or steamers.

BASIC TOOLS AND EQUIPMENT

- Hand-held can opener—get one that is sturdy and well-made.

- Corkscrew—look for the simplest and sturdiest.

- Large and small rubber scrapers—versatile and great for getting that last bit of mayonnaise out of the jar, or scraping plates.

- A medium-size stainless-steel whisk—for making a lump-free grits or cream of wheat, stirring dry ingredients, or mashing frozen orange juice.

- Two long-handled and one short-handled wooden spoons—use the longer ones for serving salad as well as stirring.

- One large and one small metal and plastic spatulas.

- A set of nesting plastic or stainless-steel bowls with plastic snap-on lids.

- A set of nesting stainless-steel measuring cups.

- Long and medium restaurant-style metal tongs—for turning food on the grill, fishing a piece of potato from the bottom of the oven, or retrieving items down in the bilge.

- Heavy, washable pot holders and heavy-duty oven mitts—very important on a boat to protect yourself from burns. Carry several in case some get wet or soaked in grease.

- One large and one small cutting board and a roasting pan or cookie sheet that can hold the large board so that you can catch the drips when you are cutting meat or something juicy.

- Large plastic colander

- Vegetable peelers

- Ice pick

- Kitchen scissors—powerful enough to cut through chicken bones and small enough to cut precisely the gills from a fish. One good design is made under the Joyce Chen label, with comfortable handles and short, pointed blades.

- Knives—see page 12.

- All-purpose box grater
- Single small-tooth grater—for small jobs
- Ladle—big enough for soup and stews

Basic Pots and Pans

- 1½-quart saucepan with cover
- 3- to 4-quart stovetop-to-oven casserole with lid
- 10-quart stock pot or kettle with lid
- 10 or 12-inch nonstick frying pan with lid
- 8-inch frying pan
- Whistling tea kettle
- Stainless-steel percolator coffeepot or plastic coffee filter holder
- Stainless-steel thermos (1- to 1½ quart)
- 12 by 18 by 1½-inch baking sheet—can serve as a tray for transferring a big fish from the cockpit into the galley, holding sandwiches and other foods as they are prepared.
- Two 9 by 9 by 2-inch non-stick metal baking pans

Non-essential, but nice to have

- 3- to 4-quart stainless-steel pressure cooker
- Electric frying pan with lid—great if you are hooked up to power at the dock

DISHES AND CUTLERY

Your options range from throwaway paper plates, cups, napkins, and plastic utensils to ceramic dishes with glassware and cutlery to match. The following "reality filters" will help you decide:

1. **Your water supply:** How much water do you have for doing dishes? Do you have a salt-water pump at the galley sink along with the fresh water tap?

2. **Cleanup demands:** How much will your crew help with dish duty? If the answer is not much, plan on meals that require fewer pots, pans, and utensils.

3. **Your itinerary:** Consider the length of your trip and your fresh water supply. If you are hopping along the coast from port to port, you may prefer disposables if you can unload your trash at each stop. On the other hand, if you are stopping frequently at marinas, you will be able to replenish your water tanks, which means more water for washing dishes and, in turn, reduce the amount of waste that you generate.

4. **Your accommodations:** Do you have room to set out dishes, or is your dining area limited to a small cockpit table?

5. **Your standards and style:** Do you like the look and feel of real plates and cutlery? Is it important to you to have the comforts of home on your boat?

6. **Your tolerance for trash:** How much do you care about contributing to the waste stream? Paper and plastic goods, while convenient, make bulky, smelly trash, and many plastics are not recyclable. Plastics and glass that are recyclable need to be rinsed and stored, then must be taken to the proper disposal area.

Many boaters use a combination of disposable dinner ware and a permanent set of dishes and cutlery, which allows for more flexibility and reduces the dishwashing burden. While real china and glassware are satisfying to use, they are not terribly practical on a boat, especially a sailboat. Whatever the boat, and no matter how watchful you are, fragile items are at risk. If you do use them, you will have to take special precautions to store them securely, protected by padding. Broken crockery or glass is particularly dangerous on a boat because shards can lodge in cracks or carpeting and resurface later to get stuck in someone's hand or bare foot.

Fortunately, options abound, both in terms of design and price for unbreakable plates, glasses, and cups that will serve you well for a long time. Marine supply stores stock specially designed plastic dinnerware with non-skid rubber feet, a feature that can be very attractive if you eat meals while bouncing around underway. Marine tableware tends to be pricey, but it will stand up to years of use. Any department or kitchen-supply store will stock a wide range of dinnerware made of plastic and a special ceramic material that is virtually unbreakable. Look for designs that include mugs and bowls that stack snugly.

Cloth napkins, a must for some on shore, are not practical on a boat, unless you have access to laundry services. Most boaters use paper. Stock up on a supply of good quality, heavy-grade ones. Cheaper, light-grade napkins are a false economy—they are not as absorbent, and, as a result, you end up using twice as many. Good quality paper towels can also double as napkins.

Insulated travel mugs and beverage cups with sealed lids and closeable openings save many a spill and are handy for both hot and cold beverages. As with dinnerware, there are many styles and models. Look for sturdy designs with wide bottoms and lids that seal securely. It is also useful to have a supply of stackable plastic glasses.

There is no law that wine must be served in stemmed wineglasses. Your guests will have a much more relaxed meal if they don't have to remain poised to lunge after a top-heavy wineglass every time a wave rocks the boat. Try the more sensible and elegant flat-bottomed straight-sided Italian-style wineglasses that are used in cafes. Many kitchen and tableware stores stock similar bistro-style faceted glasses made from break-resistant Lexan that are fairly inexpensive.

STORING: SUPPLIES, EQUIPMENT, AND TABLEWARE

Storage on a boat is at a premium. Furthermore, lockers are often out-of-the-way and getting into them can require the skills and flexibility of a contortionist. So, before you start to put away your equipment, tools, and supplies,

HAND TO MOUTH

One way to reduce the number of dishes you use is to serve foods you can eat out of hand, such as sandwiches, "wraps," pizza slices (as long as the toppings stay put), and other finger foods. This type of informal fare works well for lunch and at times when the boat is underway. Line baskets with paper napkins. Arrange the sandwiches in one and the cookies in another, then pass them around to your crew.

Organize the storage space on the boat for tools, tableware, dishes, and cooking equipment to keep them accessible and well-secured. Food items should be stored by category, to make it easier to monitor supply and condition of the food items, especially produce items kept at room temperature. Have your itinerary in mind as you organize. A motor cruise down the inland waterway may be much calmer than a fall sailing trip along the Maine coast.

think about how best to use your storage space, noting what items you will use most often. Then, after you have developed a routine and worked out any bugs, revisit the storage situation. You may realize that items you thought were absolute must-haves might be languishing unused—and taking up precious space so a little culling and rearranging might be a good idea.

In general, it makes sense to store the items you use most frequently in the most accessible lockers. Items you will use only occasionally, such as a large pot, can be tucked away into a corner and used to hold bags of chips or paper towels. Make a master list of what equipment, supplies, and other items you put in lockers, especially those that are hard to reach. Take the time to cross off non-perishable food items and supplies as you use them— especially if you are using the boat only occasionally over the course of a season. Your list will make replenishing an easy chore.

As you figure out the right storage spots for dishes, equipment, and food, keep in mind that things will shift with the boat's motion. Storage lockers should have latches or some other sort of securing device to prevent heavy objects from flying around in rough seas. Hardware or building supply stores sell inexpensive rubberized mesh for rug or tablecloth padding. Most boaters find that it's indispensable for keeping equipment and tableware steady while underway. Before you set sail, cut it to size and glue it onto the feet of bowls, platters, and other items that you want to stay put. You can also use it to line the bottom of a tool drawer, put it under a tablecloth, stuff it into a locker to wedge in an item, or use it to wrap fragile items.

GETTING READY: SHOPPING, PREPARING, AND HAULING
Before you begin your provisioning, make sure your equipment is in good working order and that refrigerators, coolers and storage lockers are clean, and mildew-free. (Don't forget to check for bugs!)

PLAN YOUR PROVISIONING

Getting ready for a week-long cruise is no small task. Make it manageable by shopping in stages. Give yourself the time you need so that transferring to the boat, unpacking, and stowing are reasonably organized. Keep in mind how the various food items will be stored on board, which items will be used first, and how you will manage the flow of food during the trip. A little advance planning, record-keeping, and anticipation will save time and trouble.

If you have the luxury of making several trips to the boat, begin by purchasing all the non-food items, canned goods, sodas, and dry foods. Repackage foods such as cereals and grains as needed (see "Trash Control" below). If you can, leave heavy, non-perishable items such as jugs of water or packs of sodas in your car or garage—don't carry them any more than you have to. Pack items in tote bags and boxes by category. A week or two ahead, prepare, package, and freeze all casseroles and meat items. A day or two before, purchase produce and perishables, repackage as needed and, if possible, refrigerate or freeze them in plastic shopping bags so that you can grab them and put them in the coolers at the last minute.

TRASH CONTROL

Experienced boaters think about trash up front, to minimize the clutter and inconvenience of handling the daily accumulation. Aside from fresh produce, most foods and other products are sold boxed, double-wrapped, or sealed in display packages. Wherever possible, reduce the amount of potential trash by removing unnecessary packaging. It is especially important to get rid of cardboard boxes, containers, and paper labels on cans because they often harbor eggs and larvae of weevils, flour moths, and cockroaches, all of which breed prolifically. Label can tops with a waterproof marking pen. If you are using cardboard boxes to transport stores to the boat, try to unpack them on deck (hose the deck clean when you are through) or unpack boxes on the dock and pass them on board

DOUBLE UP

If you are freezing casseroles and other foods in disposable foil pans, bring along a few spare pans of the same size. Set your filled pan inside the empty pan for reinforcement and to catch drips.

Pack your bread separately, in a box if possible, to protect it from getting crushed in transport. Soft fruits such as grapes, peaches, or strawberries should also be packed in rigid plastic boxes or containers.

TRAVEL LIGHT

Beverages are heavy—especially in glass containers—and glass is hard to stow safely. A six-pack of drinks in aluminum cans weighs about four-and-a-half pounds, while a six-pack in glass weighs just over seven pounds. This adds up to a lot of muscle strain if you are hauling these in and out of cars and down a long dock to the boat. Choose aluminum and plastic containers when possible.

fire-brigade-style directly into the lockers. While these precautions may seem excessive, fumigating your boat to destroy an infestation is not only unpleasant, it will involve even more work.

SMART FOOD STORAGE

High humidity and fluctuating temperatures on a boat can make it a struggle to keep food fresh and safe to eat. Packets of moisture-absorbent silica will help control excess moisture in the short term, but they are not effective for long-term use. The first line of defense against humidity is airtight containers. Purchase sturdy, reusable plastic containers for flour, grains, cereals, crackers, and cookies. They can be found in virtually any shape and size to fit your storage lockers. Pint and quart plastic deli containers are inexpensive and can be bought in quantity (by the "sleeve") from restaurant supply houses or your friendly delicatessen owner. They are versatile, long-lasting, washable, and handy for breaking down bulk items such as flour and grains into smaller sealed quantities. Use resealable plastic bags for batches of your homemade pancake mix (page 48) or bags of cake mixes slipped from their boxes (be sure to include directions). Crisp grain items such as chips, crackers, and breakfast cereals keep best if stored in amounts that will be consumed in one sitting.

If possible, do your unpacking, re-packing, sorting, and labeling at home, then transport the stores to the boat.

PACKAGED STAPLES

Buy staples with an eye towards their keeping qualities. Purchase just enough flour, sugar, cornstarch, vegetable or olive oil, salt, and other items for the duration of your trip, adding on a little extra safety margin. If you plan to use your boat all season, stock up on canned and moisture-proof vacuum-sealed foods in sizes that you are likely to consume in one meal to avoid the problem of storing leftovers. Crackers, cereal, and chips begin absorbing moisture as soon as they are taken from their packaging and will go stale overnight, but they will keep a week if well-protected in airtight containers. Put leftovers in an airtight container or zip-top plastic bag and squeeze out as much air as possible while sealing the opening.

In a tiny galley, measuring and mixing for multiple-step recipes can be overwhelming. Suddenly, packaged mixes and processed food seem very attractive. They last forever, which is helpful on long ocean passages, and many are very good. Test a few at home to see which you like best. You can also make your own pancake and corn bread mixes (page 48) at home and complete them on board. If you are planning a grilling menu, make steak and chicken marinades (page 46) ahead and store them in plastic containers. Combine them with the pre-trimmed meats you have also prepared ahead and dinner can be ready in little time.

STAPLES

Use this list as a guide to come up with your own list of staples for your boat.

FOODS:

- Pasta: Use thin varieties to cut down on cooking time.

- Instant couscous: This wheat product cooks in just a little time and makes a great substitute for rice.

- Bulgur: Processed cracked whole wheat that can be used for a pilaf or cold salad base.

- Flour: Buy a small bag for dredging or thickening if you don't plan to bake.

- Pancake mix: Buy your favorite or make your own. Package pre-measured in amounts for the size batches you plan to make, usually calculated by the number of eggs per batch.

- Canned and dried soup mixes, instant noodles

- Vegetable oil: Buy small containers for easy handling and to keep fresh. Once opened, oil goes stale, especially in warm temperatures.

- Vinegar: In addition to culinary uses, white vinegar is also useful for cleaning, degreasing (see page 23).

- Sugar and sweetener packets

TROPICAL WISDOM

In tropical climates, it is wise to take along a cooler or two for shopping trips. This allows you to pick up perishables along the way and keep them at optimally cold temperatures.

CONTAINER OPTIONS

Fish stores will sometimes sell you "fish boxes" — plastic rectangular boxes with flat snap-on lids that are used to ship fish fillets. They are versatile, stackable, and useful for keeping items dry and away from the elements. Generally, they measure 11 by 15-inches and come in 3 to 6-inch heights. Before using, run them through your dishwasher, or soak them for a few hours in a weak solution of bleach and water.

Keep a supply of versatile ingredients such as cans of tuna, pasta, tomato sauce, beans and olives for an emergency or sudden change of plans.

- Baking soda: For baking and other uses (see "Old-Fashioned Solutions" on page 23)
- Packets of instant hot cocoa and coffee and tea bags
- Powdered drink mixes
- Canned evaporated milk
- Spaghetti sauce
- Salad dressing (or vinegar and oil)
- Spices and herbs: Buy small quantities packaged in plastic containers and store in a plastic box to keep organized and protected.
- Dried onion flakes and powder, garlic salt and powder
- Canned tuna, sardines, salmon
- Canned cooked beans and baked beans
- Canned pineapple, mandarin oranges, and other fruits
- Honey, maple syrup, golden syrup
- Jam, jellies and syrups: Bring in small containers. Refrigerate after opening to prevent mold from growing on the surface.
- Peanut butter
- Cookies and crackers: Gingersnaps and plain soda crackers are good choices.
- Chips: Buy smaller bags, not giant-size.
- Canned nuts: Purchase cans with plastic lids.
- Canned smoked oysters, clams, and other seafood
- Condiments (soy sauce, ketchup, mustard, mayonnaise, hot sauce): Once opened, all but soy sauce should be refrigerated. Look for single serving packets or small containers to avoid taking partially used jars back home.
- Olives
- Water: Always have a reserve supply of drinking water in case tanks get fouled. Calculate at least ½ gallon per person per day, then add a little more to be on the safe side, especially if the weather is hot.

- NON-FOOD ITEMS:

- Heavy-duty aluminum foil
- Heavy-duty quart and half-gallon zip-top plastic bags
- Paper towels
- Waterproof ("hurricane") matches
- Glass cleaner or ammonia solution in spray bottle
- Liquid dish detergent
- Club soda (see "Old-Fashioned Solutions" below)
- Bleach (see "Old-Fashioned Solutions" below)
- Sponges
- Rubber gloves

OLD-FASHIONED SOLUTIONS

Vinegar, baking soda, club soda, and bleach are versatile and inexpensive cleaning materials.

Baking soda: It's a cleaner, degreaser, deodorizer, skin balm, and even a fire extinguisher. Put it on a damp sponge and use it as a gentle abrasive to clean waxy smudges or to scrub fiberglass, stainless-steel, and the inside of refrigerators or coolers. Take the top off a box and set it in the cooler to absorb odors. Later use it to deodorize drains or toilets by pouring down the drain and flushing with water. Sprinkle a few tablespoons on the garbage each time you add to it. Scrub grease from the grill with a paste of baking soda and water. Use this same paste to soothe insect bites or rashes. Keep a box near the stove to douse a grease fire.

White vinegar: Use it as a good all-purpose cleaner. Mix it with an equal amount of water to wipe down kitchen and bathroom surfaces or to remove mildew and soap scum. Use straight to clean windows or to soak off labels or decals.

Club soda: Pour it directly on wine-stained carpet or clothing, rub in and sponge off. Pour or spray on, then wipe to shine counters, stainless-steel, and greasy surfaces.

Bleach: Use a solution of 1 tablespoon chlorine bleach and 1 gallon of cool water to dip citrus fruits for longer storage, to disinfect coolers, toilets (heads), cutting boards, and other surfaces. Use in very dilute amounts to disinfect water supply.

TRASH MANAGEMENT AND DISPOSAL

One more word about trash: Eliminate as much as you can beforehand. Liquids such as cooking oil, sauces, and beverages come in cans, glass, plastic, and laminated plastic and foil boxes. On-shore disposal of these items is generally convenient in U.S. and European waters, but it can be problematic in less developed areas.

While it is tempting to think the sea is vast enough to absorb your small bag of trash, marine pollution is a serious problem, which is exacerbated by individual acts of dumping. U.S. and international regulations require that nothing be dumped overboard within three miles of a coastline. Beyond the three-mile limit, items that can be dumped overboard include food scraps, paper, glass, and metal that are broken down in very small pieces—less than one inch.

Tossing trash, bottles, and cans overboard in an anchorage or within the three-mile limit is the worst breach of boating etiquette. They are unsightly and dangerous to swimmers and people on shore. Glass bottles carried by tides and currents eventually end up broken on the shoreline, posing a hazard to people, pets, and wildlife.

Plastic trash of any kind must be held on board for disposal on shore. Even so-called biodegradable plastics take months of exposure to ultra-violet light before they break down. Since most plastics float, they pose a hazard to sea creatures that mistake them for food. Many birds, fish, turtles, and other sea animals die from ingesting plastics or from becoming entangled in them. In addition, floating plastics can become entangled in boat propellers and engine water intakes.

Playing It Safe

KEEPING FOOD SAFE

Whether you are at home or in your boat galley, keeping food safe involves two basic principles:

1) Temperature Control
2) Cleanliness

Most food poisoning is caused by bacteria that have multiplied to dangerous levels on foods. These organisms are present throughout the environment, but they are threatening only when conditions are right. Meat, especially if raw, is most often the vector of food-borne illness.

Most bacteria will not multiply at temperatures below 40°F or above 140°F. The range in between is called the "danger zone" because these temperatures are ideal for rapid bacterial growth. For example, bacterial levels on food left out in 90°F temperatures can reach toxic levels in one hour.

Proper cleanliness and handling will prevent the spread of bacteria. First, isolate raw meat or poultry by enclosing it in plastic bags to prevent juices from dripping onto other foods in your refrigerator. Wash hands thoroughly before and after handling raw meat or poultry. After using utensils (including grilling utensils) on raw or partially cooked meat or poultry, wash them in hot, soapy water before using again. Bacteria can survive for long periods on counters and

If your boat's refrigerator and freezer run on an electrical system, you have to be careful about times when you leave the boat and it shuts off. If you're gone for an hour or two, there's no need for concern. But if you're away for the day, check to make sure your food stayed cold while you were gone. Here's a simple method: Put an ice cube in a small cup and place it in the freezer. Check the ice in the cup when you return. If it has melted and refrozen into a flat shape, then the power was off long enough to cause everything to defrost. Meat items should be thrown out as they are probably spoiled.

cutting boards, and especially on sponges and dish cloths. Sanitize these items daily with a weak solution of bleach and water. Rinse well before using again.

KEEPING IT COOL

Maintaining foods at the proper temperature and keeping drinks cold requires daily monitoring. The trick is to keep all the items inside your marine icebox organized, easy to find, protected, and, most importantly, at the correct temperature. Bring a refrigerator thermometer to help you keep an eye on the how well the box is holding the cold.

The more often the box is opened, the faster it will lose its chill, causing food to spoil faster. If you let people dive into the icebox for drinks and snacks, the box will lose its cool quickly. And, in a top-loading box, since everything is packed vertically, you'll also have a jumbled mess on your hands. The solution—bring a separate portable cooler aboard to keep on deck or in the cockpit. This allows the crew to graze on snacks any time they like, while keeping them out of your icebox!

The next step to food safety is creating a system that keeps the food both accessible and protected from getting crushed or saturated with melt water. Following a few common sense rules will help:

1. Store the same types of items in the same place.

2. Keep heavier items such as cartons of milk at the bottom of the box and lighter, fragile items such as lettuce on top.

3. Put highly perishable meat and seafood in waterproof plastic containers or resealable plastic bags and cover with bags of ice. (Or pack and freeze as described on page 28 or in the sidebar on page 21.)

4. Once beverage containers are opened, keep them upright to prevent spills, or transfer them to bottles or pitchers with secure lids.

As the ice melts, water collects at the bottom of the icebox. Allow a few inches to remain in the box to help hold the cold and slow down the rate at which the ice melts. Most ice chests have a drain at the bottom to draw off excess water. It can get clogged with a leaf or soggy food label. Minimize the problem by keeping as many items as possible in plastic bags, preferably transparent.

With a deep icebox, you can't help unpacking it to get what you need at the bottom. While you may have an incredible memory, it is easier to label frozen and refrigerated items, especially items in opaque packaging. Use a wax pencil to mark the tops of plastic containers with the name and date to help you decide what to use first.

To eliminate chaos, cluster items by category. Keep groups of items in rigid plastic containers or heavy plastic bags. When you need to get to the bottom of the icebox, you can lift out whole groups, then replace them. If practical, make temporary shelving with larger square plastic containers by setting them on top of a foundation of equal-sized objects such as containers of yogurt or jugs of milk.

As mentioned before, it is a good idea to segregate drinks and snacks in a separate cooler to conserve the cold in the icebox and make it easy for crew members to get what they need. Keep non-perishable beverages in a locker in the bilge—usually the coolest storage outside of the icebox. In colder waters, tie drinks in a mesh bag and suspend them overboard for a few hours. Finish off beer and soda in the ice chest if you want them refrigerator-cold, but no additional chilling is required for white wine.

You will need a good supply of ice to maintain your icebox and supplemental coolers. Block ice and cube ice are commonly available, and it is helpful to use a combination of both. Block ice lasts longer, while cube ice helps fill in spaces around items, especially in a chest cooler, and for putting into drinks. When you are packing the cooler, try to place the ice as high up in the chest as you can so that the cold is distributed as evenly as possible.

ICE ON ICE

Fill clean plastic jugs with water, leaving an inch or more of air space at the top for expansion, and freeze them solid. Set them upright in the cooler. When they have melted, use the cold water to drink.

MANAGING PERISHABLES

MEAT, POULTRY AND FISH

Meat, poultry, and fish are highly perishable and must be kept very cold. They spoil faster in a cooler or icebox than in a home refrigerator because the temperatures are not as constant. For that reason, limit fresh items to what you will use in a day or two. Salted items such as processed meats or deli ham last a little longer because of the preservatives, but still must be kept as cold as possible. If you are not using meat and fish the day of your arrival on the boat, bring them to the boat as cold as possible, even frozen.

Depending on the shape and size of your icebox, you may find it helpful to pack items such as frozen meat inside of a plastic box with a snap-on lid. If you have the room in your home freezer or have access to a commercial freezer locker, you can make efficient use of your boat's icebox by following these steps when freezing meat: Wrap each portion in plastic wrap, then lay pieces flat in a labeled resealable plastic bag. Lay bags in freezer box, adjusting pieces of meat to fill each layer evenly. Overlap bag edges so that you can grasp them easily for removal. When the box is full, freeze overnight or until frozen solid.

MILK AND DAIRY PRODUCTS

For shorter trips, if you have the room, bring the same quantity of milk that you consume at home, but purchase it in smaller containers, preferably plastic. Store the containers upright in the bottom of the cooler. Mark the top of the one that is currently open and keep it in the part of the icebox that will be disturbed least when you take it out. Yogurt will keep much longer than fresh milk because it is cultured. To retard mold growth on semi-soft and hard cheeses, wrap them in paper toweling that has been heavily sprinkled with vinegar and then wrung out. Store in plastic bags or plastic containers. Store sticks of butter or margarine in rigid airtight plastic containers to keep them from absorbing odors from the icebox and from getting waterlogged.

BREAD

When you buy bread for a trip, keep in mind that it will go moldy very quickly unless it is made with preservatives. Freshly baked breads, even dense, sourdough types, will mold faster on a boat. Pita bread, which stores conveniently flat, tends to last longer and is versatile. It can be used for pocket sandwiches or to make savory chips. Simply cut into triangles, toss with herbs and a little oil, and bake until golden.

For the short term, the best way to store bread is to wrap it in a plastic bag and keep it in a cool, well-ventilated area or in a dry spot in the icebox. A string hammock is helpful for storing breads out of the way and protecting them from crushing. Some long-distance boaters wrap their bread in a cloth that has been splashed with vinegar and wrung out. Check your bread daily by sight and smell for mold. If you see a few spots, simply cut them off and use the bread. Stale bread can be turned into other dishes such as French toast, grilled sandwiches, bread pudding, cinnamon toast, or croutons for salad.

EGGS

Eggs can be stored for up to two weeks unrefrigerated in a cool spot if they are very fresh when you get them. Specially designed plastic egg holders that latch shut are a good investment and can be purchased in camping and boating stores. They are convenient for storing eggs safely in crowded lockers. Some supermarkets sell eggs packaged in clear rigid plastic containers, which will work almost as well. To check an egg for freshness, place it in a bowl of water. If it floats, discard it—it is far past its prime.

KEEPING PRODUCE FRESH

Fruits and vegetables are very much alive and continue to "breathe," or respire, even though they have been cut from the plant they grew on. As they take in oxygen, they give off carbon dioxide and in the process the plant tissue changes and eventually deteriorates. Produce such as soft

SLIPPERY TRICK

Eggs can be kept for up to month unrefrigerated if they are sealed with a thin film of petroleum jelly to exclude air. Just make sure you have a good grip on the eggs so they don't slide out of your hand!

As fruit ripens, it gives off ethylene gas that speeds up ripening. For that reason, many fruits such as bananas and tomatoes are picked green and then exposed to ethylene to ripen them before sale. When you want to ripen fruit quickly, you can harness the ethylene given off from such fruits as apples or bananas. Put the fruit to be ripened in a paper bag with a ripe banana or apple. Close the bag loosely and put in a warm place for a day or two. Leave a small opening in the bag to allow the oxygen to get in and the carbon dioxide to escape.

lettuce deteriorates faster than grapes or potatoes. And the riper the produce, the faster its deterioration.

The ideal way to preserve most produce is to keep it cold and humid and to reduce its oxygen supply, or, in other words, wrap it in plastic and keep it refrigerated. Chances are that after packing your milk, butter, and meats, you won't have much room in your icebox for produce. Since lettuce is most perishable, it should be refrigerated first. The rest of your fresh produce will have to be stored at the ambient temperature (see page 32). Some types will keep for a long period of time without refrigeration if you follow a few guidelines:

1. In general, fresh produce items should be kept as cool as possible in a well ventilated area that allows easy access for inspection. These items should be checked daily to make sure they are secure and unspoiled. Cull spoiled items, and pull items that should be used first.

2. If you are fortunate enough to have access to a farmers' market, you will find that absolutely fresh produce has a longer shelf life than that sold in supermarkets, which may be several weeks old by the time you buy it. Whatever the source, select vegetables that are firm, fresh and free of bruising. Fruits should be purchased in varying degrees of ripeness so that they will be ready in stages.

3. If you plan to store produce at room temperature that has previously been refrigerated, let it come to ambient temperature in a cool dry place and blot away surface moisture before wrapping and storing.

You can extend the life of vegetables stored at room temperature even further by using a new type of storage bag called Evert-Fresh®. Made from a finely perforated film impregnated with a mineral that absorbs ethylene gas, the green bags reduce the moisture that hastens mold and rot. Although they are intended for refrigerated storage, the bags also work well at room temperature. As a rule of thumb, at moderate temperatures, the perforated bags will increase the storage life of vegetables by about one-fourth. The bags can be used several times if carefully washed and dried between uses. For more information contact the company at www.greenbags.com.

The spot you select for storing fresh fruits and vegetables should be dark, cool, dry, well-ventilated, and easy to reach. Each item should be stored securely to prevent it from rolling and bruising. Use "breathable" containers that you can lash down securely, such as milk crates or plastic baskets. Wrap items individually in paper towels or newspaper (you can re-use the paper towels). The cardboard forms used to layer apples in boxes work well for tomatoes and other fruits. In rough weather, it is a good idea to keep a length of netting on hand to fasten over the top of your stash to keep it from banging and bruising. String hammocks work well as long as they swing free, and are also handy for storing bread and bags of crushable bags of chips. Make sure your produce is dry when you store it; moisture is the enemy and will hasten mold and rot.

Lettuce is great to have for salads and sandwiches, but if you prefer the leafy varieties to iceberg, it is best to prepare them ahead to minimize storage space and the water needed for washing. Wash the lettuce well in cold water, then drain and blot dry on cloth toweling. Stack the leaves gently, wrap in several sheets of paper toweling to absorb excess moisture and store in a resealable plastic bag. Squeeze out as much air as possible when sealing the bag and refrigerate. Excluding the oxygen will greatly extend its storage life. Lettuce prepared this way will stay fresh at least a week if kept cold.

Check your fruits and vegetables daily and remove any with mold or rot immediately or the spoilage will spread. As an item ripens, serve it or keep in the icebox in a plastic box to keep away fruit flies, which will drive you crazy if they get established.

SOME LIKE IT HOT

Many tropical and semi-tropical fruits and vegetables are harmed by refrigeration and will rot once they get cold. Never refrigerate tomatoes, as it destroys the flavor. Likewise, bananas will turn black and stop ripening if chilled.

FRUIT AND VEGETABLE UNREFRIGERATED STORAGE TIMES

The times given below are calculated based on very fresh, high quality produce that has not been washed and will be stored at approximately 70° F. You can increase the storage life by about a quarter by using the Evert-Fresh® bags described on page 30. Starred items are unripe.

Vegetable or Fruit	Days at Ambient Temperature
Apples	5–10
* Avocados	10–12
Broccoli	1
Cabbage	21
Cantaloupes	10
Carrots	7–10
Citrus fruit (lemons, oranges, grapefruit)	10
Grapes	3
Green beans	1
Green peppers	5
Onions	40–60
* Peaches	5
* Pears	5–10
Potatoes (Russet or baking)	40–60
Summer squash (yellow and zucchini)	5
Winter squash (hard-shelled)	90
* Tomatoes	10–15
Watermelon (Sugar Baby, a small variety)	14

* Purchased unripe, a ripe fruit will not last as long. A ripe avocado, for example, will hold for just 6 or 7 days.

Safety Tips

Here are some suggestions for easy ways to work safely in your galley:

✓ Keep a cutting board secure by setting it on top of a damp towel or damp sponge cloth.

✓ Fill pots no more than half-way with liquids and, if possible, secure lids to pots when you are cooking underway.

✓ Steam, rather than boil vegetables. (This also helps conserve energy and water.)

✓ When you are preparing food underway, anything that is loose can become a projectile. Keep sharp knives, tools, or the raw ingredients you plan to use in the galley sink.

✓ Use the sink to hold cups, thermoses and other containers that you are filling with liquid.

✓ Keep the galley floor grease-free. Have on hand a spray bottle of ammonia and water (or glass cleaner) and a sponge dedicated to the job of wiping down the galley floor after each meal.

BE CAREFUL COOKING UNDERWAY

No matter how much you try to anticipate danger in the galley, cooking underway is always unpredictable. Consider the story of a woman, a sailor and sailing cook with many miles of racing under her belt. One evening, while on a sailing passage to Bermuda, she decided to cook linguine with marinara sauce. Being a smart, experienced sea cook, she had precooked the linguine and had it heating in the oven under foil wrapping in an oiled pan, with some bread tucked alongside. On top of the gimbaled stove, she put a pot half-filled with the sauce on to heat and snugged on the fiddles to hold it tight. All was bubbling along and she ducked into the saloon to get some napkins. At that moment a freak wave hit the boat broadside. The sauce shot from the pan in an arc, splashing the cabin from top to floor, and then oozed into a locker of cookies and ran down into the bilge. She was unharmed, but it was a white pasta dinner that night, and she spent the rest of her voyage and return removing oily orange Marinara sauce from "everywhere," she said. This won't happen to you if you remember two rules. First, don't cook liquids while underway. Or, if you must, place a small amount in a large pot, so it's less likely to spill.

STOVE SAFETY

Boats come with two types of stoves—gas and alcohol. The gas may be either natural gas or propane. Regardless of the fuel, all must be operated properly for safety's sake. Gas especially, is explosive, and needs to be handled with care. Before setting sail, read the manufacturer's manual that comes with your stove and keep it on board for reference.

If your stove uses natural cooking gas, it will be stored in canisters that are linked to the stove with a hose and connectors. There are shut-off valves at the tank and stove. Make it a habit to shut off the fuel when the stove is not in use. Check the connectors regularly to make sure they are not leaking: With the gas on, brush the junction of the hose and the connector with soapy water. If it bubbles, shut off the gas, tighten the connector and test it again. Natural gas does not give as hot a flame as propane, but it has a safety advantage—the gas dissipates up and out of the cabin when there's a leak.

Propane is more desirable because it burns hotter than natural gas, but it is more dangerous because it is heavier than air and sinks. Consequently, it is critical that you don't let it leak and accumulate in your boat's bilge. A tiny spark can cause a big explosion. A good propane system will have a remote on-off switch that cuts the fuel off at the tank and can be operated from the galley. It should also include a gas "sniffer" that closes the gas switch if it senses gas in the air. The control knobs on propane stoves should be the type that have to be pushed in before they can be turned to ensure that they are not accidentally turned on if you knock up against them in rough seas. Finally, the stove should have a sensor that shuts off the fuel if the flame is blown out. Test your stove before embarking to make sure it's operating safely.

The advantage alcohol stoves have over gas is that an alcohol flame can be doused with water. However, they are finicky, hard to light, and require constant monitoring to avoid accidents. The reservoir of an alcohol stove should be refilled only in calm conditions, because the alcohol is easy to spill and may ignite accidentally. An alcohol flame is invisible in direct sunlight, so it's hard to gauge how high the heat is when you're cooking. If an alcohol stove is your only option, it is wise to invest in an alternative cooker, such as a portable burner, just in case.

Gas and alcohol stoves both have pilot lights that must be lighted and kept lit in order to ignite the main flame. Newer models have built-in igniters that make it much easier and safer to light the stove. If your stove doesn't have one, you might want to invest in a mechanical or an electronic stove lighter, which makes a tiny spark that will ignite the stove fuel. Designed to be used one-handed, they are much more convenient and cleaner to use than matches.

GRILLING SAFETY

Everyone loves dinner cooked on the grill, and on a hot day, it will save you from turning your galley into an inferno. Kettle-shaped stainless-steel marine grills can be mounted on the transom of your boat. Some models come with stands so that you can use them on shore. A few common sense tips will help you grill successfully and safely.

- Never grill while underway. You don't want hot coals flying about.

- Don't cook on a super hot fire, or if flames are still visible. If you can't hold your hand above the grate for more than two or three seconds, the fire is too hot. Let it cool down a few minutes before you put the food on.

- Make sure the grill is clean. As the grill heats, or the fire burns down, set the rack over the flame and use a wire brush to scrape off any residue from a previous cook-out.

- Oil your food very lightly. Too much oil will cause a flare-up and give your food an off-taste.

- Keep a spray bottle of water nearby to put out flare-ups. A thin stream of water directed at the flame will take care of the problem without dousing the entire fire.

- Watch for attacks from the air: In well-traveled areas, seagulls have learned to associate humans and boats with food. These aggressive birds are capable of snatching the steak off the grill if you leave it unattended.

- Watch for wakes: When you are in a busy anchorage, stay close to your grill when the food is on. If someone drives by too fast, creating a big wake, you'll be able to save your dinner.

- Store charcoal in a heavy plastic bag both to keep it dry and contain the black dust. Dedicated grillers can invest in a specially made charcoal bag that zips closed.

Planning Ahead

When planning your meals aboard, keep in mind that you are there to enjoy sailing, not the confines of a galley. Food preparation (including clean-up, trash management, and juggling storage) takes much longer on a boat, and tasks that are simple on land become challenges on the water. So, to ensure great meals with minimal fuss, prepare as much as you can at home and streamline before setting sail.

PREPARATION TRADE-OFFS: TIME, PERISHABLES, & REFRIGERATOR SPACE

For quick meals, include a supply of "instant" foods in your galley pantry. Canned stews, soups, and crackers are perfectly acceptable boat food and are great to have on hand for a fast, hot meal in a hurry. However, for good eating, you will want to do some of your own preparation. Besides fully prepared dishes, you can make life easier by finishing even small tasks ahead. Cook a dozen hard-cooked eggs, peel a head of garlic and a few onions to last the week, package the dry ingredients for pancakes (see page 48), and shape and freeze hamburger patties.

The size and dependability of your boat's refrigeration space will determine the amount of perishables you bring. Chances are, you'll be juggling a small icebox and one or

FRESH FIRST, CANNED LAST

Plan your menus so that you are using up the most perishable items first, and keep canned and packaged foods on hand both for back-up meals and for the last meals of the trip.

two portable coolers. To maximize cold storage, balance menus with make-ahead favorites and shelf-stable convenience foods. Bring only the amount of perishable foods you expect your crew can consume. If your itinerary includes multiple stops at places where you can replenish perishables such as milk and meats, then you will have more room in the cooler for other, hard-to-find perishables.

PREPARING AHEAD

FRESH PRODUCE

To reduce preparation time and garbage, you can partially prepare many fresh fruits and vegetables ahead and either cook or reheat them on board. You can also purchase packaged pre-cut fruits and vegetables in the supermarket, or pre-cut items from your farmers' market yourself. "Fresh-cut" produce, a wonderful and convenient alternative to canned vegetables, is often processed with preservatives for longer shelf life. Select these items with care, as they are more costly and not as fresh as unprocessed produce.

A few common sense rules will apply when you are bringing along pre-cut fresh produce. In general, the firmer the vegetable or fruit, the better it will keep when it is cut or pre-cooked. Once you have cut or peeled a fruit or vegetable, it will begin to deteriorate faster, even under refrigeration. To prepare fresh produce that will last a few days in the icebox, follow these steps:

- Choose the freshest produce possible, with minimal bruising.

- Take extra care to prepare food on clean surfaces, including cutting boards and knives.

- When pre-cooking vegetables, cook them in plenty of rapidly boiling salted water until crisp-tender and chill immediately under cold running water, then drain well. Reheat them by sautéing or steaming in a pan, or serve them cold, tossed with a dressing.

- Use resealable plastic bags for storage, and press out excess air before sealing.

- Refrigerate fruits and vegetables immediately after preparing.

- Package fruits and vegetables in amounts that will be consumed in one sitting. Avoid leftovers!

- Place cut fruit such as cantaloupe or pineapple in rigid plastic containers to protect from bruising. It will keep on ice or in an icebox for a few days.

- Plan to consume soft fresh fruits such as strawberries, figs or raspberries at one meal. They are too delicate to store successfully.

- To save cooking time, steam or boil scrubbed potatoes until they are just barely tender and plunge them into cold water to stop the cooking. Toss them with a little oil and cook on the grill, brown in a frying pan with onions, or add to a soup or stew. If you want to have your favorite potato salad, make it ahead. It will keep for several days in an icebox. But if your recipe calls for hard-cooked eggs, bring them along separately and add them at the last minute.

- Prepare hard-cooked eggs ahead, but don't peel. They will keep for at least a week, but once they have been peeled, they should be eaten within a day.

- Peel and chop fresh garlic cloves to use on board. Store in an airtight plastic container in the icebox.

- Peel whole onions and store in an airtight plastic container (to prevent odors from permeating other items). They will keep for a week. Don't chop onions in advance because chopped onions develop an off taste and tend to spoil quickly.

- Buy roasted peppers in jars instead of preparing them at home. Freshly made, they tend to spoil very quickly unless they are doused with vinegar.

MEAT, POULTRY, AND FISH

Highly perishable foods, such as meat, poultry, and fish, should be stored in the coldest part of the icebox at a temperature of 38°F. Meat and poultry should be consumed within a few days. Fresh fish should be eaten the day it is purchased. If you aren't planning to use an uncooked meat item within a few days, freeze it beforehand for 24 hours in the coldest freezer you can find (0°F or colder is ideal).

As cooking in a galley is tricky, do whatever you can to prepare meats ahead and avoid the smelly, messy task of dealing with them on the boat. When buying meat for

QUICK RECIPE

Sauté ground
meat with onion
and garlic and
use for a pasta
sauce or chili;
or add capers,
olives, and tomato
sauce to make a
picadillo, and
serve with rice.

your trip, choose boneless cuts and do any necessary trimming beforehand. Save the T-bone steak for land and try a flank steak instead. If you have access to a supermarket with a complete meat counter or a good butcher, it will be an easy task to get your meats ready for your trip. Use boneless chicken breasts and beef, pork, or lamb cut into steaks or scallops. Meat chunks are good for shish kebabs.

After preparing the meat, wrap each portion in plastic wrap. Make a label for each package using freezer tape or a mailing label (sheets of labels for laser printers work well) and mark with waterproof ink. Note the name of the item and the date you are freezing it. Then place the packages inside a large resealable bag, fitting as many as will fit in one layer, then press out the air as you seal the bag. Freeze packages flat so that they will pack compactly. For a very neat and tidy solution, find a plastic box with a flat lid that will fit into the icebox. Pack the plastic bags in the box and freeze. In addition to containing the dripping meat juices, this method provides an insulating effect that will help lengthen the time that the items stay frozen.

Shape ground meats such as beef, lamb, pork and turkey into patties in advance, then wrap them individually and freeze. Ground meats, because they are processed more than whole cuts of meat, should be handled with particular care and used as soon as possible. If your frozen ground meats have thawed, cook them right away.

You can also save time by marinating meat or poultry that you plan to have in the first day or two and store it in a spill-proof plastic container or freezer-weight resealable plastic bag (see page 46 for some marinade recipes). In addition to tenderizing and adding flavor, marinades with acid ingredients such as vinegar or seasonings such as chiles and black pepper have a mild preservative effect that help extend the refrigerated life of fresh meat. However, never marinate fish ahead of time. It is already tender, and a stay beyond an hour in an acid marinade will toughen the flesh.

BREAD AND GRAIN BASICS

Bread does not last well on a boat because humid, warm conditions cause it to become moldy in a short time. You can extend its life by keeping it in the icebox, and by transforming it into other dishes when it loses its freshness. (See page 29 for tips on keeping bread as fresh as possible.) If it gets stale, don't despair. There are creative ways to use it up. Here are a few ideas:

There's the old favorite—French toast. Or you can make a bread pudding by soaking stale bread in beaten eggs and milk, then adding a little cinnamon and sugar. Place mixture in a buttered baking dish and pour over extra custard just to barely cover bread. Cover dish and bake at 350°F for about 45 minutes. Another option is a French-style sandwich: Place slices of ham and cheese between two slices of bread. Dip in an egg/milk batter and fry in a little butter or oil until golden on both sides.

Fried stuffing is yet another possibility. Tear up enough bread to make 3 cups and put into a bowl. Sauté about ½ cup of chopped onion in butter or oil. Add chopped ham or sausage if you have it. Add to bread with a beaten egg. Season with herbs, a little powdered chicken bouillon, garlic salt, and hot sauce. Add milk, a tablespoon at a time, to moisten, but don't let it get soggy. Fry it in one big cake or individual cakes in butter or oil in a non-stick skillet until brown. Turn and brown the other side. This homely dish is delicious, satisfying, and adaptable.

PREPARING FOOD IN ADVANCE

SANDWICHES

The first day out on the boat is always a little disorganized, as everyone settles in. For a smooth transition, make your meals for that first day ahead, so that all you will need to do is pop down into the galley to heat the food.

Sandwiches fit the bill for lunch on board, as long as they are simple, and can be held and eaten with one hand. As to type of sandwiches, submarine sandwiches work well on a boat, as they can be assembled all at once, and cut into portions. Make sandwiches at home and wrap individually in plastic, then keep cold until you are ready to serve. For best results, use firm breads and avoid juicy fillings. You can add something juicy like a tomato slices (slice them at home and bring in a plastic container) or a little coleslaw just before serving, but make sure it won't cause the sandwich to fall apart or become unwieldy.

DESSERTS AND SNACKS

If you are baking loaf cakes, bars, brownies, or other sweets, slice them ahead of time to avoid cutting on the boat. Wrap carefully in foil or plastic to preserve freshness. Homemade muffins and bakery goods will keep a day or two unrefrigerated, while commercial products tend to last longer because they usually contain preservatives.

PASTA

If you want to avoid waiting for water to boil for cooking pasta (especially shapes such as penne that take longer to cook), boil some ahead of time, but just until it is barely done. Drain the pasta immediately, then toss with olive or vegetable oil, season if desired, and cool completely before storing. Pre-cooked pasta can be stored in plastic containers or resealable plastic bags in the icebox for a few days. To reheat, put it in a large pan with a few tablespoons of water and oil, cover and heat gently until hot, or simply add it to your simmering sauce.

FREEZING AND REHEATING

On a boat, food should be tasty, easy on the digestion, and above all, familiar. Unless you and your crew are seasoned sailors, being on a boat can be a little disorienting, or even disconcerting, and a comforting home-cooked meal is a simple, powerful antidote. For the cook, make-ahead casseroles are terrific boat food—they involve minimum time in the galley and do not demand delicate handling. Most of the dishes that fall under the "comfort" heading— macaroni and cheese, beef stew, shepherd's pie and chicken soup—also take well to freezing and reheating.

Add a lettuce or vegetable salad and bread or potatoes and you have a complete, satisfying meal.

For ease of serving on board, pre-cut substantial baked dishes such as lasagne and moussaka into portions. To save time and trouble in the galley, package the casseroles as follows: Use a disposable aluminum pan or an oven-proof casserole dish made from non-breakable ceramic or metal that fits in your boat's oven. Coat the pan thoroughly with non-stick vegetable spray. Prepare the casserole and layer it in the prepared pan. When the casserole is cooked, cool it completely and refrigerate. Cut the chilled casserole into portions in the pan. If you are using a foil pan, be careful not to cut through the foil. Or to be extra careful, invert the casserole onto a cookie sheet, cut into portions while keeping the pieces together, then fit the pan back on top and invert the casserole back into the pan. Cover the pan with foil. Put the whole thing in a large plastic bag, secure the end with a tie, and freeze.

To defrost, place frozen casserole in the icebox for 8 to 12 hours before reheating. The casserole will thaw, while at the same time add a little extra cooling power to the icebox. NOTE: A defrosted casserole should be cooked within 12 hours of defrosting.

In addition to casseroles, homemade meatloaf is a make-ahead treat that satisfies the toughest of snarling sailors. It must be flavorful and juicy, which means a light hand with the breadcrumbs and a sufficient amount of fat. Chilled meatloaf slices easily and makes great sandwiches, hot or cold (see page 68). For hot sandwiches, reheat slices of meatloaf gently in tomato sauce or barbecue sauce.

VERSATILE FOUNDATIONS: BASIC RECIPES TO BUILD ON

If you have been sailing all day and have a hungry crew to feed, homemade tomato sauce will be cause for celebration. Just add a few embellishments to turn it into a main course. The recipe that follows is a foundation that can be used in many different dishes. It can be a base for a fish or chicken chowder dressed up with chunks of bell peppers and potatoes, or a sauce in which to reheat leftover meatloaf slices. Even more options follow the recipe below.

Tomato Sauce

Makes about 4 cups

3 tablespoons olive oil
1 large onion, finely chopped
4 cloves garlic, minced
1 (28 ounces) can tomatoes, coarsely chopped
    with their juice
2 tablespoons tomato paste
¾ teaspoon dried rosemary, crumbled
¾ teaspoon salt
¼ teaspoon cayenne pepper
½ cup chopped fresh basil or parsley

In a large skillet, heat oil over medium heat. Add onion and garlic and cook 10 minutes, stirring frequently, or until onion is golden. Stir in tomatoes, tomato paste, rosemary, salt, and cayenne and bring to a boil. Reduce to a simmer, cover and cook 10 minutes. Stir in basil.

VARIATIONS

Quick Jambalaya: Add 1 to 1½ cups of cooked rice to sauce along with cooked sausage and ham. NOTE: Don't add uncooked rice to the sauce. It will take too long to cook because of the acidity of the tomatoes.

Chicken Sausage: Add 12 ounces of chicken sausage and simmer for 10 minutes, or until done. Once cooked, slice the sausages.

Ham: Stir in 1 cup diced ham. Simmer to heat through.

Shrimp: Add 12 ounces medium-size peeled and deveined shrimp. Cook 3 minutes, or until just cooked through.

Fish: Add 1 pound skinless, boneless cod, cut into 1-inch chunks and cook 5 minutes, or until cooked through.

EMBELLISHMENTS

For a quick supper, while you heat the water to cook some thin spaghettini, put the sauce in a pan to heat and toss in a can of chickpeas (drained), a cup of olives, and seasonings. Serve with grated Parmesan or crumbled feta, breadsticks, and raw vegetables, and dinner is ready.

Creamy Sauce Base

Makes 7 cups

5 tablespoons unsalted butter
1½ cups coarsely chopped onion
1½ cups coarsely chopped celery
½ cup diced carrot
5 tablespoons all-purpose flour
4 cups milk
1 cup clam juice or chicken broth
1 cup heavy cream
½ teaspoon salt
¼ teaspoon black pepper

Melt the butter in a 4-quart pot. Stir in vegetables and sauté for 5 minutes. Add the flour and cook, stirring, for 3 minutes. Remove from heat.

Pour in milk and clam juice, stirring constantly, until smooth and blended. Return pot to heat and bring to a boil, stirring constantly. Simmer for 3 minutes. Stir in the cream and salt and pepper. Let cool, then cover and chill or freeze.

Add seafood and/or other vegetables and, if desired, a little white wine to soup when reheating.

A creamy sauce base can morph into a chunky cheesy potato vegetable chowder, a sauce for baked chicken, a base for creamy ham and biscuits, or salmon and pasta casserole. The base recipe is rich, but you can lighten it by using non-fat milk or a combination of low-fat milk and defatted chicken broth.

When cool, sauce or base may be poured into resealable plastic bags designed for liquids and frozen in small batches.

T
I
P

The marinades and mixes that follow add home-cooked flavor with minimal galley time.

Steak Marinade

Makes about 1 cup, enough for 2 pounds of meat

2 tablespoons dark brown sugar
⅓ cup freshly squeezed lime juice
1 teaspoon grated lime zest
1 teaspoon grated fresh ginger
1 tablespoon Worcestershire sauce
3 tablespoons Teriyaki sauce
1 teaspoon hot pepper sauce
2 tablespoons Dijon-style mustard
1 clove (more to taste) garlic, minced
¼ cup dry red wine
¼ cup olive oil
¼ teaspoon coarsely ground black pepper

In a bowl, dissolve brown sugar in lime juice. Stir in zest, ginger, and Worcestershire, Teriyaki, and hot pepper sauces. Beat in mustard, garlic, and wine. Then beat in oil. Season with the pepper. Pour into a 1-quart (or larger depending on how much steak you plan to marinate) resealable plastic bag.

TIP

For day trips, place steaks or chicken in bag with marinade before leaving home and carry in a cooler. For overnight trips, pack steaks or chicken and marinade separately. About 4 hours before grilling, slip steaks or chicken into bag with marinade. Reseal. Turn bag several times during marinating.

Chicken Marinade

Makes about ½ cup, enough for 2 pounds of chicken

1 cup dry white wine
3 tablespoons freshly squeezed lemon juice
Grated zest of 1 lemon
1 tablespoon soy sauce
3 green onions (white and light green parts), thinly sliced
1 clove garlic, minced (optional, but suggested)
Salt and freshly ground black pepper
3 tablespoons olive oil
2 tablespoons chopped fresh cilantro (see TIP)

In a bowl, combine wine, lemon juice and zest, soy sauce, green onions, and garlic. Season well with the salt

TIP

For a longer trip, chicken marinade can be frozen, but cilantro should not be added until marinade has thawed.

and pepper. Beat in oil and stir in cilantro. Pour into a 1-quart resealable plastic bag (or larger depending on how much chicken you plan to marinate) .

Spice Mixes for Grilled Fish

2 teaspoons coarsely ground black pepper
1 teaspoon freshly grated lemon zest
½ teaspoon ground ginger
1 teaspoon ground coriander
1 teaspoon sugar
Pinch teaspoon ground red pepper
¼ teaspoon ground allspice
1 teaspoon coarse salt
OR
1 teaspoon coarsely ground black pepper
1 tablespoon fennel seeds, lightly crushed
1 teaspoon ground cloves
1 tablespoon ground cinnamon
1 tablespoon whole star anise

To use, sprinkle over both sides of fish fillets, pressing it in to ensure it sticks. For grilling whole fish, make diagonal slashes in both sides of fish. Sprinkle spice mix over skin and into slashes. Grill as usual.

T
I
P

For either mix, combine ingredients in a glass jar or plastic container with a tight fitting lid. Shake to mix.

Herb-Garlic Vinaigrette

Makes 1¼ cups

¾ cup extra-virgin olive oil
6 tablespoons red wine vinegar
1 tablespoon Dijon-style mustard
3 cloves garlic, minced
¾ teaspoon dried oregano
¾ teaspoon dried basil
¾ teaspoon salt
Freshly ground black pepper to taste

An all-purpose vinaigrette is great to have on hand. Use it for salads, and also try it drizzled over grilled vegetables, on sandwiches, or as a marinade for chicken or beef.

In a large jar with a tight fitting lid, combine oil, vinegar, mustard, garlic, oregano, basil, and salt and shake until well combined. Store in the refrigerator/cooler.

Pancake Mix

Makes 3½ cups of mix, enough for 2 batches

½ cup powdered buttermilk
2 cups all-purpose flour
1 cup whole-wheat flour
¼ cup granulated sugar
2 teaspoons baking powder
1 teaspoon baking soda
½ teaspoon salt

In a large bowl, whisk together all ingredients until well blended. Store in an airtight container at room temperature. See page 126 for ideas on mixing batter.

Corn Bread Mix

Makes an 8-inch square cake

⅓ cup yellow cornmeal
1 cup all-purpose flour
¼ cup granulated sugar
5 tablespoons powdered buttermilk
1½ teaspoons baking powder
½ teaspoon salt

In a bowl, whisk together all ingredients until well blended. Store in an airtight container at room temperature. See page 128 for ideas on mixing batter.

SPECIAL ADDITIONS: CONDIMENTS, SAUCES, AND OTHER EMBELLISHMENTS

After a long day of sailing, there is nothing nicer than a home-cooked meal. But if the weather fouls up your plans, a few emergency stores will allow you to produce a meal in a hurry. As long as the food is tasty, people won't mind that it's not entirely homemade. Staples that will save the day include cans of tuna, tomato sauce, thin pasta, canned beans, beef stew, canned soups, and instant noodles. Add a few herbs and spices, and you can serve up a meal that everyone will appreciate.

Most supermarkets carry special condiments and sauces that can help you enliven meals with no fuss—anchovy paste, horseradish, capers, pickled vegetables, pesto, flavored oils and vinegars are a few ideas. Buy small quantities of these items for easier storage and packing. Here are a few favorites that work well on a boat

- Hummus—Many supermarkets sell 8- and 16-ounce containers of hummus, also known as chickpea spread. Try it on a sandwich garnished with chopped olives, grated carrot, shredded cabbage, and chopped onion; serve as a dip with chips, vegetables, or pita bread. Or, serve as a side dish with grilled chicken or meat.

- Sun-dried tomatoes, capers, olives, and other salty, vinegary condiments enhance chicken salads and tuna salads and add a kick to pasta sauces and dips.

- Pesto or olive paste can be used as a condiment for grilled chicken or fish, or with pasta or potatoes. Mix pesto with mayonnaise for a sandwich spread or tuna or chicken salad.

- Pre-grated cheeses are worth the cost for the convenience. Use them to dress up a salad, scatter on a flour tortilla in the frying pan for a quesadilla, or sprinkle on scrambled eggs.

- Canned salsa is great served with tortilla chips for a snack or as a sauce for a scrambled egg and tortilla breakfast. For a quick and spicy dinner dish, simmer it with boneless chicken breasts, or for a fast chili, simmer it with sautéed ground beef (or turkey) and canned pinto or black beans.

- Mango chutney transforms chicken salads, especially if you sprinkle in a little curry powder. Or mix with mayonnaise or yogurt and curry powder for an easy dip for vegetables or shrimp. Serve it as a condiment for grilled pork. Chop any large pieces of chutney and thin with a little white wine and use the mixture to glaze ham steaks.

- Miso is a flavorful, nutritious bean paste that is a staple of Japanese cooking. It can be used in soups, salad dressings, and marinades. Look for it in Asian markets and natural foods stores.

- Polenta rolls, tubes of an Italian cornmeal mixture, are found in the dairy section of large supermarkets. Use it in place of rice or pasta as a base for pasta sauces or chili, or fry rounds in a little butter and sprinkle with cheese for a delicious side dish.

MENU PLANNING AND SHOPPING

A carefully thought-out menu plan is well worth the time. It will help you organize shopping and will ensure the cook is not unnecessarily burdened with food preparation. It will even help you cut down on trash.

Use the menus that follow as a guide for how you might go about planning meals for a few casual parties as well as a two- or three-day trip. All the menus use a combination of make-ahead and prepared foods to supplement dishes that are prepared underway. You'll want to fill in with some special snacks. The result is delicious, varied meals with on-board preparation time, waste, and trash kept to a minimum.

Shopping lists are provided for the first few menus. They will give you a way to think about your marketing and develop a system.

MENU PLANNING FIRST STEPS

Whatever your menus, follow a few preliminary steps to save time and have a more enjoyable cruise.

✓ When planning your menus and snacks, keep in mind the equipment and the amount of storage space (especially cold storage) available on board.

✓ Consider the ages of your crew and any special dietary needs or preferences.

✓ If any crew members enjoy cooking, think about assigning some of the make-ahead dishes to them.

✓ Check your inventory of staples (both foods and cleaning supplies) and replenish as necessary. Don't forget to check your supply of sealable plastic bags, foil pans, and other paper products.

✓ Figure out your beverage needs and add them to your shopping list.

✓ After your shopping is done, remove all excess packaging and/or repackage foods as necessary.

Day Trip

Barbecue

Gazpacho (page 78)

Bread sticks

Grilled Pork Tenderloin (variation, page 82)

Grilled Vegetables (page 70)

Buttered steamed potatoes

Fruit and cookies

Strategy:

PREPARE COMPLETELY AHEAD:

Gazpacho

Cookies (or purchase)

PARTIALLY PREPARE AHEAD:

Grilled pork— marinate meat

Grilled vegetables—wash and cut into serving pieces ahead

PURCHASE:

Bread sticks

Fruit

PREPARE UNDERWAY:

Buttered steamed potatoes

Grilled pork and vegetables— grilling step only

Shopping List

Tomato juice

Onions

Garlic

Cucumbers

Peppers

Tomatoes (optional)

Red wine vinegar

Olive oil

Salad dressing

Bread sticks

Pork loin

Marinade ingredients

Potatoes

Fruit

Cookies

HINTS

- Make the gazpacho ahead of time and keep on ice up to 24 hours in advance. The vinegar in the soup will help preserve the vegetables. Serve the gazpacho in mugs for sipping to minimize dishwashing.

- The meat can be put into the marinade the morning of the dinner. If it is frozen, take it out the night before, put it in the marinade in a sealed plastic container and keep in the icebox for up to 24 hours. As the meat defrosts it will pick up the flavors from the marinade.

- Keep bread sticks crisp by packaging in resealable plastic bags in amounts that will be eaten at one sitting (figure four to five pieces per person depending on the size of the breadsticks) and keep bags inside an airtight plastic container.

- Grill extra vegetables for sandwiches the next day.

Afternoon Cruise

Cool Weather Supper

Cincinnati Chili (page 84)

Crunchy Vegetable Salad with Maple Vinaigrette (page 111)

Apple Crisp (page 136)

Strategy:

PREPARE AHEAD:

Chili (and pasta if desired)

Maple Vinaigrette

Vegetables for salad such as shredded carrot, chopped cucumber, and bell pepper

PURCHASE:

Garnishes for chili—shredded cheese and chopped olives

PREPARE UNDERWAY:

Apple crisp

Heat chili

Combine vegetables and vinaigrette

Shopping List

Ground beef

Spaghetti

Canned tomato sauce or canned tomatoes

Garnishes for chili

Onions

Garlic

Herbs and spices

Vegetables for salad (canned and/or fresh)

Maple syrup

Apples

Graham crackers

Orange marmalade

HINTS

- Freeze the chili ahead and defrost 24 hours ahead in the icebox.
- While chili is heating, prepare the vegetable salad using vegetables such as chopped bell peppers, cucumbers, and red onions.
- If you like, top the crisp with a little vanilla yogurt.
- If you have leftover salad, refrigerate it. The next day, add some chopped deli ham and serve it for lunch.

Two-day Cruise

First day out

Lunch:

Pre-made sandwiches

Everything Cookies (page 131)

Dinner:

Shells with Little Meatballs (page 85)

Green salad with Herb-Garlic
vinaigrette (page 47)

Italian or French bread

Strategy:

PREPARE AHEAD:

Sandwiches

Cookies (or purchase)

Shells with Little Meatballs (or partially
prepare ahead)

Garlic-Herb Vinaigrette

PARTIALLY PREPARE AHEAD:

Wash greens for salad

PURCHASE:

Italian or French bread

PREPARE UNDERWAY:

Finish sandwiches if desired

Reheat shells

Toss salad

Shopping List*

Bread (sandwich and French
or Italian)

Luncheon meats

Cheese

Condiments

Chocolate chips and other
cookie ingredients

Pasta shells

Ground beef

Onion

Garlic

Canned tomatoes or tomato
sauce

Grated Parmesan or Romano
cheese

Broccoli

Eggs

Milk (fresh, shelf-stable or
canned)

Butter or margarine

Herbs and spices

*Shopping list for additional
ingredients needed for second
day continues on page 52.

HINTS

- If you have a farmers' market in your area, buy your salad greens there. They will usually be fresher, which means they will last longer.

- If you like to add sliced tomatoes or similar ingredients to your sandwiches, do so just before serving. Otherwise, sandwiches will get soggy.

- Buy a little extra Italian bread and save it to use for French toast (see menus for second day out, page 54).

Second day out

Breakfast:

French toast

Lunch:

Salmon Salad (page 103)

Bulgur and Lentil Salad (page 108)

Pita wedges

Dinner:

Grilled Chicken with Couscous (page 90)

Cantaloupe Salsa (page 62)

Rice or couscous

Warm Chinese Broccoli Salad (page 110)

Chocolate Date-nut Bars (page 138)

Strategy:

PREPARE AHEAD:

Bulgur and Lentil Salad

Cookies (or purchase)

Marinade for chicken

Cantaloupe Salsa

Chocolate Date-nut Bars

PARTIALLY PREPARE AHEAD:

Warm Chinese Broccoli Salad (see Hint)

PURCHASE:

Pita bread

PREPARE UNDERWAY:

French toast

Salmon Salad

Complete broccoli salad

Rice or couscous

Marinate chicken and grill

Shopping List (continued)

Yogurt

Cinnamon

Maple Syrup or pancake
syrup

Canned salmon

Horseradish

Cucumbers

Onions

Celery

Lettuce or cabbage

Fresh broccoli

Mayonnaise

Bulgur

Dry or canned lentils

Salad dressing

Boneless chicken breasts

Cantaloupe or other melon

Lime juice

Red onion

Hot red pepper flakes
or fresh chili

Rice or couscous

Sesame oil

Soy sauce

Vegetable oil

HINT

• For the broccoli salad, cook broccoli ahead and chill. Just before serving, toss with dressing. Marinating broccoli too long turns it an unappealing color.

Three-Day Cruise

First day out

Breakfast:
Cereal
Fruit

Lunch:
Pasta with Chickpeas (page 107)
Cookies

Dinner:
Chicken Enchiladas (page 89)
Melon spears

Strategy:

PREPARE AHEAD:
   Chicken Enchiladas
   Melon spears

PARTIALLY PREPARE AHEAD:
   Pasta with Chickpeas

PURCHASE:
   Cookies
   Cereal and fruit

PREPARE UNDERWAY:
   Finish Pasta with Chickpeas

HINT

- Mix wheat or oat bran flakes with a granola-type cereal before you leave home and bring it on board in an airtight plastic container. If you don't want to bother with fresh fruit, use raisins or dried cranberries instead.

Second day out

Breakfast:
Tropical Fruit Sundaes (page 124)

Lunch:
Tuna salad in pita pockets
Chips and pickles

Dinner:
Pot Roast Plus (page 80)
Bread
Raw vegetable sticks
Cherry-Chocolate Brownies (page 130)

Strategy:

PREPARE AHEAD:
   Granola and fruit for sundaes
   Tuna salad
   Pot Roast Plus
   Cherry Chocolate Brownies

PURCHASE:
   Raw vegetable sticks
   (or prepare ahead)
   Chips and pickles
   Pita pockets and bread

PREPARE UNDERWAY:
   Assemble sundaes
   Assemble sandwiches

HINT

- Tuna salad can be enhanced in a number of ways. Besides the usual hard-cooked eggs and celery, try chopped apple, carrot, or olives, as well as grated onion or a little mustard. Or try the recipe on page 69.

Third day out

Breakfast:
Buttermilk Pancakes (page 126)

Lunch:
Hot or Cold Pot Roast Sandwiches
  (page 69)
Marshmallow Crème Fudge (page 137)

Dinner:
Vegetarian Lasagne (page 98)
Three-bean salad
Bread
Warm Sautéed Bananas (page 135)

Strategy:

PREPARE AHEAD:
  Marshmallow Crème Fudge
  Vegetarian Lasagne

PARTIALLY PREPARE AHEAD:
  Pancake Mix

PURCHASE:
  Bread
  Three-bean salad

PREPARE UNDERWAY:
  Cook pancakes
  Pot roast sandwiches
  Sautéed bananas

HINT

- Dress up pancakes by adding chopped fruit, leftover from the sundaes, to the batter.

- If you have leftover vegetable sticks from the previous night's dinner (from the second day), chop them and add them to the bean salad for extra crunch.

Appetizers & Snacks

Taking it easy is part of what recreational boating is all about. Snacks on hand to pass around to a hungry crew and a repertoire of easy appetizers you can whip up at day's end take the pressure off the cook at mealtimes. And while it's great to have a stash of cheeses, crackers, nuts, olives, and the like, without much more effort you can offer all kinds of tempting, homemade treats, or add a personal touch to packaged staples.

Most of the recipes in this chapter are multipurpose. What works as a dip in the evening makes a tempting sandwich spread at lunch the next day. Some recipes that serve eight people in appetizer mode can become main dishes for four. We've offered suggestions for other ways to use the recipes and any leftovers, but don't be limited by them. Let your imagination be your guide.

As you turn the pages of this chapter, you'll find some recipes for cool-weather cruises, like Hot Spinach and Feta Dip, and others for warm summer days—when a platter of cool Shrimp Ahoy fits the bill perfectly. Kids and grown-ups alike will love the Tomato-Avocado Salsa, Brie and Apricot Quesadillas, and Trail Mix Deluxe. They're sure to become family standards on land and sea.

IN THIS CHAPTER

Tomato-Avocado Salsa

Sun-dried Tomato Spread

Yogurt-Garlic Dip

Lemony White Bean Dip

Cheddar-Sardine Spread

Sesame-Tahini Sauce

Mediterranean Herb Spread

Bean and Salsa Dip

Warm Spinach and Feta Dip with Olives

Cantaloupe Salsa

Shrimp Ahoy

Sweet and Sour Kielbasa

Trail Mix Deluxe

Marinated Olives

Brie and Apricot Quesadillas

Pickled Pepperoncini

Tomato-Avocado Salsa

This versatile dip makes a delicious omelet filling. Use the remaining avocado half as a garnish or on Meatloaf Sandwiches (page 68).

Makes 2 cups
Prep time: 15 minutes plus standing

2 large ripe tomatoes, seeded and diced, or 4 canned
    tomatoes, diced
1 small red onion, diced
2 scallions (including green tops), chopped
2 garlic cloves, finely chopped
½ avocado, peeled and cut into small pieces
¼ cup chopped fresh cilantro or parsley
1 tablespoon fresh lime juice
1 teaspoon olive oil
1 teaspoon minced and seeded fresh or pickled jalapeño
    pepper, or ¼ teaspoon hot red pepper sauce

In a medium bowl, stir together all ingredients gently but thoroughly. Cover bowl loosely with plastic wrap and let stand at room temperature for 30 minutes to allow flavors to blend. Cover any leftovers tightly with plastic wrap and refrigerate. Serve with tortilla chips.

Sun-dried Tomato Spread

Mix leftovers with mayonnaise for a delicious sandwich spread.

Makes 1 cup
Prep time: 10 minutes

3 tablespoons prepared pesto
3 tablespoons fresh lemon juice
⅓ cup olive oil
2 small fresh or canned tomatoes, finely chopped
2 scallions (including green tops), finely chopped
1 (8-ounce) jar oil-packed sun-dried tomatoes, drained
    and finely chopped

TIP

If you don't have oil-packed tomatoes, soak dried tomatoes in boiling water for 30 minutes. Pat dry and proceed as directed.

In a bowl, whisk together the pesto, lemon juice, and olive oil. Stir in the fresh or canned tomatoes, scallions, and sun-dried tomatoes. Serve with pita wedges or water crackers.

Yogurt-Garlic Dip

Makes 1½ cups
Prep time: 10 minutes plus standing
Cooking time: 5 minutes

2 cups plain low-fat yogurt
8 cloves garlic, peeled
¾ teaspoon dried oregano, crumbled
½ teaspoon salt
¼ teaspoon black pepper
¼ cup minced red onion

Place yogurt in a fine-meshed sieve set over a bowl. Let drain, refrigerated, for 4 hours or overnight.

Meanwhile, in a small pan of water, boil the garlic for 2 minutes. Drain and cool, then finely chop.

In a medium bowl, stir together drained yogurt, garlic, oregano, salt, and pepper. Fold in red onion. Serve with crisp vegetables or potato chips.

Draining the yogurt makes a thick, rich dip, but that step can be omitted. Or you can drain it at home before you leave.

This dip tastes best made a day ahead and refrigerated. It allows more time for flavors to blend.

TIP

Lemony White Bean Dip

Makes 1½ cups
Prep time: 10 minutes

1 (15-ounce) can white kidney beans, rinsed and drained
3 tablespoons olive oil
1 teaspoon grated lemon zest (optional)
2 tablespoons lemon juice
½ teaspoon salt
¼ teaspoon ground red pepper
¼ cup plain yogurt or sour cream
⅓ cup oil-packed sun-dried tomatoes, drained and finely
    chopped, or 2 tablespoons sun-dried tomato paste

In a large bowl, combine beans, olive oil, lemon zest, lemon juice, salt, and red pepper. With a potato masher or the back of a large spoon, mash the beans until chunky. Stir in yogurt and sun-dried tomatoes. Serve with sliced French or Italian Bread.

If you don't mash the beans, this recipe becomes a great salad.

Sun-dried tomato paste comes in tubes and can be found in large supermarkets.

TIP

Cheddar-Sardine Spread

For five minutes' work, you get a flavor-packed spread. You can also use the spread as a filling for grilled cheese sandwiches or quesadillas.

Makes 2 cups
Prep time: 5 minutes

1 (3¾-ounce) can oil-packed sardines, drained
8 ounces shredded cheddar or Monterey Jack cheese
   (about 2 cups)
1 clove garlic, minced or pressed
¼ cup chopped fresh parsley

In a bowl, mash sardines with a fork. Stir in cheese, garlic, and parsley. Serve cold with water crackers or spread a little on toasts and bake at 400°F, or broil until cheese is melted and bubbly.

Sesame-Tahini Sauce

This sauce can be made ahead and brought on board. Use it as a dip for breads or crackers or pour it over warm vegetables.

Makes 1½ cups
Prep time: 10 minutes plus chilling
Cooking time: 2 minutes

½ cup tahini paste or smooth peanut butter
¾ cup warm chicken broth
2 cloves garlic, finely minced or pressed
⅛ teaspoon granulated sugar
1 teaspoon freshly grated ginger (optional)
1 teaspoon grated lemon zest
3 tablespoons fresh lemon juice
⅛ teaspoon ground red pepper, or more to taste
2 tablespoons sesame oil
Salt and black pepper to taste

TIP

Look for tahini paste in health food stores or the imported foods section of large supermarkets.

Stir tahini paste into warm broth until well blended. Beat in remaining ingredients. Cover and refrigerate several hours or overnight. Bring to room temperature and beat well before serving.

VARIATION

For sesame noodles, toss sauce with hot cooked pasta and sprinkle with peanuts or toasted sesame seeds before serving.

Mediterranean Herb Spread

Makes 3 cups
Prep time: 10 minutes

3 large scallions, cut into 1-inch lengths (including green tops)
3 garlic cloves
1 (8-ounce) package cream cheese, softened
4 ounces plain or herbed feta cheese, crumbled
1 stick (½ cup) unsalted butter, softened
2 teaspoons dried herbs de Provence (see TIP)
Freshly ground black pepper to taste
Chopped black olives for garnish

Place the scallions and garlic in a food processor. Pulse several times until coarsely chopped. Add the remaining ingredients, except olives, and process until the spread is smooth and creamy. Transfer to serving dish and garnish with olives. Serve with toasts or crackers.

Bean and Salsa Dip

Makes 2 cups.
Prep time: 5 minutes

1 (15-ounce) can pinto beans, rinsed and drained
2 tablespoons olive oil
1½ teaspoons chili powder
1 teaspoon ground cumin
1 teaspoon ground coriander
1 cup mild to medium salsa
2 scallions, thinly sliced (optional)

In a medium bowl, combine pinto beans, olive oil, chili powder, cumin, and coriander. With a potato masher or large spoon, mash beans until mostly smooth with some chunks. Stir in salsa and scallions, if using. Serve with corn chips.

ROSEMARY

Use any leftovers as a sandwich spread. It will take a roast beef sandwich to another realm.

You can substitute ½ teaspoon each dried thyme, oregano, marjoram, and rosemary for the herbs de Provence.

TIP

For a treat, spread some dip on tortilla chips and sprinkle with grated cheese. Bake or broil until cheese is melted.

Warm Spinach and Feta Dip with Olives

Warm pita triangles or juicy cherry tomatoes make great dippers.

Makes 3 cups
Prep time: 20 minutes
Cooking time: 15 minutes

1 (8-ounce) package cream cheese, softened
4 ounces feta cheese, crumbled
½ cup mayonnaise
2 teaspoons fresh lemon juice
1 (10-ounce) package frozen chopped spinach, thawed and
    well drained
4 ounces Kalamata (or any Greek) olives, pitted and chopped
½ red onion, chopped

Preheat the oven to 400°F. Lightly grease a 1-quart baking dish. In a medium bowl, stir together cheeses, mayonnaise, and lemon juice until well blended. Stir in spinach, olives, and onion. Transfer mixture to prepared baking dish. Bake until bubbly, about 15 minutes.

VARIATION

To cook on top of the stove, omit mayonnaise. Heat 2 tablespoons olive oil in a large skillet over medium heat. Add onion and cook, stirring, until softened. Reduce heat to medium-low. Stir in remaining ingredients and cook until blended and heated through.

Cantaloupe Salsa

This salsa makes an excellent topping for cheese quesadillas or an accompaniment to grilled meats or fish. If you prefer, substitute honeydew melon for the cantaloupe.

Makes about 3 cups
Prep time: 15 minutes plus chilling

2 cups finely diced cantaloupe (about ½ a large melon)
3 tablespoons fresh lime or lemon juice
⅛ teaspoon crushed red pepper flakes
2 tablespoons finely chopped onion
2 tablespoons olive, canola, or other vegetable oil
Salt and freshly ground black pepper to taste
¼ cup chopped fresh mint, or 1 teaspoon dried mint (optional)

Stir together all ingredients in a medium bowl. Transfer to a plastic container with a tight-fitting lid. Refrigerate several hours or overnight. Stir again before serving.

Shrimp Ahoy

Serves 6–8
Prep time: 20 minutes plus marinating

½ cup fresh lemon juice
¼ cup vegetable oil
1 tablespoon red wine vinegar
2 cloves garlic, crushed
1 tablespoon dry mustard
2 teaspoons salt
½ teaspoon paprika
Ground red pepper to taste
1 bay leaf
1 lemon, thinly sliced
1 small red onion, thinly sliced
2 tablespoons chopped fresh parsley (optional)
2 pounds cooked shrimp, peeled and deveined

In a large bowl, whisk together lemon juice, oil, vinegar, garlic, mustard, salt, paprika, and red pepper. Stir in the bay leaf, sliced lemon, red onion, and parsley. Add shrimp and toss well to coat. Marinate in the refrigerator for 2 to 4 hours. Remove the bay leaf, then drain shrimp and arrange on a serving platter.

For a special presentation, serve the shrimp on wooden skewers with 1/4-inch-thick cucumber rounds, which have been marinated with the shrimp for about 30 minutes.

On the boat, you can do all of the mixing for this recipe in a resealable plastic bag.

TIP

Sweet and Sour Kielbasa

Serves 6
Prep time: 5 minutes
Cooking time: 20 minutes

16 ounces turkey kielbasa, cut in ½-inch-thick rounds
1 (12-ounce) bottle chili sauce
1 (10-ounce) jar apple jelly
1 tablespoon spicy or Dijon-style mustard
Juice of 1 lemon

Place a large skillet over medium-high heat. Add kielbasa and cook, turning occasionally, for 10 minutes. Pour off any excess fat. Reduce heat to low. Add chili sauce, jelly, mustard, and lemon juice and combine. Simmer, stirring, for 10 minutes. Cook until heated through. Transfer to a heat-proof dish and pass with toothpicks.

Packed with flavor, these hearty bites are made for cool evening snacking. Serve with extra mustard on the side for dipping.

Trail Mix Deluxe

Pass this snack around all day long. Make up a batch at home and bring it on board in an air-tight plastic container. In a pinch, it makes a great breakfast.

Makes 8 cups
Prep time: 15 minutes
Cooking time: 10 minutes

1½ cups natural (unblanched) almonds
1½ cups dried apricot halves, cut into ½-inch chunks
1½ cups pitted dates, cut into ½-inch chunks
¾ cup raisins or currants
¾ cup hulled pumpkin seeds
1 (6-ounce) bag semisweet chocolate chips

In a large skillet over medium heat, toast the almonds, stirring frequently, until fragrant and crisp, about 7 minutes. Remove from the pan and when cool enough to handle, coarsely chop. Transfer to a large bowl.

Add the apricots, dates, raisins, pumpkin seeds, and chocolate and toss to combine.

TIP

A good pair of scissors makes cutting dried fruit a breeze.

Marinated Olives

For extra color, use a mix of green and black olives.

Makes 2 cups
Prep time: 15 minutes plus 1 week to cure

2 cups green or black oil-cured olives
6 (2-inch) strips lemon zest
3 cloves garlic, peeled and lightly crushed
⅔ cup olive oil
3 tablespoons fresh lemon juice
¾ teaspoon dried rosemary
¼ teaspoon fennel seeds
¼ teaspoon salt
¼ teaspoon crushed red pepper flakes

TIP

Reserve the left-over oil mixture from the olives and use it in a salad dressing or toss it with pasta.

With the flat side of a large knife, lightly crack each olive. Place olives, lemon zest, and garlic in a clean, dry jar or plastic container. In a medium bowl, whisk together oil, lemon juice, rosemary, fennel seeds, salt, and red pepper flakes. Pour mixture over olives and refrigerate for at least a week to allow flavors to develop.

Brie and Apricot Quesadillas

Serves 6
Prep time: 10 minutes
Cooking time: 15 minutes

½ cup dried pitted apricots
2 ounces brie cheese
6 (8-inch) flour tortillas

If apricots seem dry, soak for 15 minutes in boiling-hot water to cover. Pat dry and cut into small dice. Cut the brie into small pieces. (You should have about ½ cup.) Top one tortilla with about one-third of the brie and one-third of the apricots. Cover with a second tortilla. Repeat with remaining apricots, cheese, and tortillas.

Lightly oil a griddle or skillet. Place over medium-high heat. Place quesadilla on griddle and cook for about 4 minutes, turning once. Cut into wedges and serve. Cook remaining quesadillas as directed.

VARIATION

For a hearty lunch, add a slice of ham to each quesadilla. Serve one quesadilla per person.

The best way to eat these quesadillas is hot off the griddle. Make them in batches instead of all at once. To save time on board, soak and chop the apricots at home.

If you don't have dried apricots, use 1 teaspoon of apricot jam per quesadilla. Spread on tortillas before adding brie.

T
I
P

Pickled Pepperoncini

Pepperoncini are thin red Italian peppers. Serve this jazzed up version alongside crackers and cheese or in place of pickles with sandwiches.

Makes 2 cups
Prep time: 5 minutes plus chilling

⅔ cup olive oil
3 tablespoons red wine vinegar
¾ teaspoon dried oregano
½ teaspoon salt
2 cups pickled pepperoncini
6 (2-inch) strips lemon or orange zest
4 cloves garlic, peeled and lightly crushed

TIP

Pepperoncini can be made up to 2 weeks ahead and refrigerated.

In a medium bowl, whisk together oil, vinegar, oregano, and salt. Place pepperoncini, lemon zest, and garlic in a clean, dry jar or plastic container and pour oil mixture over. Refrigerate at least overnight to allow flavors to develop.

Soups & Sandwiches

T he sun is high in the sky and it's time for lunch! Whether your crew has had a busy morning trimming the sails or just watching for navigation aids, their appetites are beginning to peak. If you've been cruising for a while, you've no doubt exhausted your menu of routine canned soups and lunchbox-type sandwiches. Ready for some new, quick-and-easy, delicious ideas?

Most of the recipes in this section are either easy-to-assemble time savers or soups that are worth making ahead and just reheating. And, if you've already made the meatloaf on page 83 or the pot roast on page 80, the Meatloaf Sandwiches and the Hot Pot Roast Sandwiches will be a snap. Serve cheese quesadillas with the Fog Horn Chowder with Ham, and you'll have a meal that's hearty enough for dinner.

Is there a nip in the air? Try the Chunky Potato-Cheese Chowder or the Bean Soup with Tortillas. Too hot to cook? How about a Creamy Shrimp Bisque or a delicious Chunky Gazpacho made with V-8 juice. Kids on board? Try the hot Peanut Butter Soup or Peanut Butter and Bacon Sandwiches. All of these are sure to please your hungry crew.

Peanut Butter and Bacon Sandwiches

Cook extra bacon for breakfast and save it to make these sandwiches for lunch.

Serves 4
Prep time: 10 minutes

½ cup creamy or chunky peanut butter
8 slices firm white or whole-grain sandwich bread, toasted
8 slices cooked bacon
1 large Granny Smith apple, cored and thinly sliced
8 romaine or iceberg lettuce leaves (optional)

Spread peanut butter on each slice of bread. Top 4 slices of bread with bacon and apple slices. Top each with 2 lettuce leaves. Place remaining bread, peanut butter side down on top of the lettuce. Serve.

Meatloaf Sandwiches

Use the other half of the avocado to make the salsa.

Serves 4
Prep time: 10 minutes

Tomato-Avocado Salsa (page 58)
8 slices home-made style white or whole-grain bread
2 tablespoons Dijon-style or other mustard
4 slices leftover meatloaf (page 83)
½ avocado, peeled and thinly sliced
leaf lettuce or thinly sliced onion (optional)

Generously spread salsa on 4 slices of bread and set aside. Spread remaining bread slices with mustard. Top with the meatloaf and avocado slices. Cover with lettuce. Top with remaining slices of bread and serve.

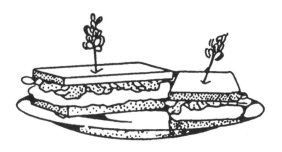

Hot Pot Roast Sandwiches

Serves 6
Prep time: 5 minutes
Cooking time: 10 minutes

6 generous slices pot roast (page 80)
1½ cups leftover pan juices and vegetables from pot roast
6 Kaiser rolls

Combine the meat, pan juices, and vegetables in a medium skillet and cook gently over low heat until heated through, about 8 minutes.

Meanwhile, preheat broiler. Split Kaiser rolls and place, cut sides up, on a baking sheet. Run under broiler until just toasted. Transfer split rolls to serving plates and top each with warm meat and vegetable mixture.

Hearty and filling, these sandwiches are a meal in one. If you prefer, skip the cooking and broiling and serve the sandwiches cold— they're delicious either way

Tuna Pita Melts

Serves 4
Prep time: 15 minutes
Cooking time: 10 minutes

1 (6-ounce) can oil-packed tuna, drained
3 scallions, chopped
4 ounces Monterey Jack cheese, shredded (about 1 cup)
1 (12-ounce) can artichoke hearts, drained and chopped
¼ cup chopped black olives
¼ cup mayonnaise
3 tablespoons mild salsa
4 pita pockets

If serving the sandwiches hot, preheat oven to 350°F.

In a medium bowl, combine tuna, scallions, cheese, artichoke hearts, and olives. Stir in mayonnaise and salsa.

Open pita pockets at one edge and stuff each with about one-quarter of the tuna mixture. Wrap sandwiches in foil and bake (or heat in skillet over low heat) until heated through and cheese is melted, about 10 minutes.

You can make the tuna salad ahead and heat and assemble the sandwiches once you're underway. In warm weather, serve the sandwiches cold.

Grilled Vegetable Sandwiches

If you're grilling vegetables for dinner, cook extras for these sandwiches and marinate them overnight in salad dressing. Or grill the vegetables at home and transport them in the marinade, ready to put on rolls.

Serves 4
Prep time: 15 minutes plus marinating
Cooking time: 10 minutes

1 small to medium eggplant, cut lengthwise in
     ¼-inch slices
4 medium Portobello mushroom caps
1 green bell pepper, seeded and
     quartered lengthwise
1 red bell pepper, seeded and quartered lengthwise
2 small zucchini, cut lengthwise in ¼-inch slices
1 Vidalia or other sweet onion, sliced into
     thick rounds
3 tablespoons olive oil
Salt and black pepper to taste
1 cup Herb-Garlic vinaigrette (page 47)
     or bottled vinaigrette
4 crusty Kaiser or submarine rolls

Arrange vegetables in a single layer on a large baking sheet. Brush with olive oil on both sides and lightly season with salt and pepper.

Preheat grill or broiler. Place vegetables in a grill basket, directly on the grill, or on a broiler pan. Grill or broil, turning carefully from time to time, for 10 minutes, or until vegetables are lightly charred and crisply tender.

T I P **If you like, use bottled hoagie or submarine sandwich dressing in place of vinaigrette.**

Remove vegetables from the grill or broiler. Place all vegetables in a large sealable plastic container or bag. Drizzle with half of the vinaigrette. Let vegetable mixture cool completely, then seal container or bag and refrigerate overnight.

To serve, split rolls lengthwise, and, if possible, grill or toast lightly. Remove mushrooms from container or bag and slice in half. Divide the vegetables, including mushrooms, among 4 roll halves. Drizzle with remaining vinaigrette. Top with remaining roll halves and serve.

Fog Horn Corn Chowder with Ham

Serves 6
Prep time: 20 minutes
Cooking time: 30 minutes

4 slices thick bacon
1 large onion, chopped
2 tablespoons all-purpose flour
2 (14- to 16-ounces each) cans reduced-sodium
    chicken broth
4 medium red-skinned potatoes, diced
2 cups milk
2 (15 ounces each) cans corn, drained
1 pound smoked ham steak, cut into cubes
Freshly ground black pepper to taste
Snipped chives or scallion tops for garnish

In a large pot over medium heat, cook the bacon until almost crisp. Remove bacon and drain on paper towels. Let cool, then chop into small pieces and set aside. Drain all but 2 tablespoons of drippings from the pot. Add onion to pot and cook over medium heat, stirring, until tender. Add the flour and cook, stirring, for 3 minutes.

Stir in the chicken broth and diced potatoes. Simmer until potatoes are tender, about 10 minutes. Add milk, corn, ham, bacon pieces, and pepper. Cook, stirring occasionally, until heated through, about 5 minutes. Ladle into bowls or mugs and sprinkle with chives or scallion tops.

VARIATION

For longer trips, this chowder can be prepared with canned ham or canned Danish bacon, canned or long-life milk, chicken bouillon such as Knorr-Swiss, and dried chives.

If you're making this at home, use frozen baby white corn in this soup— it's especially delicious. For a filling lunch or supper, serve with cheese quesadillas.

Chunky Potato-Cheese Chowder

When the weather gets cool, bring out the soup pot. For a luscious supper, serve the soup with grilled sausages or stir in some chopped ham, bacon, or smoked turkey.

Serves 4
Prep time: 15 minutes
Cooking time: 30 minutes

1 tablespoon olive oil
1 large onion, cut into ½-inch chunks
2 cloves garlic, minced
1½ pounds all-purpose potatoes, peeled and cut into
    ½-inch chunks
1 (14- to 16-ounce) can chicken broth, or 2 bouillon
    cubes mixed with 2¾ cups water
½ teaspoon salt
½ teaspoon black pepper
⅛ teaspoon grated nutmeg (optional)
¾ cup milk
4 ounces shredded cheddar cheese (about 1 cup)

In a large saucepan, heat the oil over medium heat. Add the onion and garlic and cook, stirring frequently, until the onion is softened, about 10 minutes.

Stir in potatoes, broth, salt, pepper, and nutmeg and bring to a boil. Reduce heat to low and simmer, covered, until potatoes are tender, about 15 minutes. Remove from the heat. With a potato masher or fork, mash about one-third of potatoes against the side of the pot. Stir in milk and cheese. Return pan to the heat and simmer until soup is hot and cheese is melted, about 3 minutes.

Miso Soup

This warm, fragrant soup can be made in an instant. Serve it for lunch with sandwiches or as a snack on a cool afternoon.

Serves 4
Prep time: 10 minutes
Cooking time: 5 minutes

2 teaspoons vegetable oil
2 cloves garlic, minced
1 tablespoon peeled and minced fresh ginger
2 tablespoons miso paste (preferably light, like shiro miso)
4 teaspoons soy sauce
1 tablespoon granulated sugar

¼ teaspoon salt
3 cups boiling water
1 tablespoon dark sesame oil (optional)
2 scallions, thinly sliced, or 2 tablespoons freeze-dried chives

In a medium saucepan, heat the vegetable oil over low heat. Add the garlic and ginger and cook for 2 minutes, stirring frequently until the garlic is tender. Stir in the miso paste, soy sauce, sugar, salt, and water and return to a boil. Boil for 1 minute. Stir in the sesame oil and scallions and serve.

Thai Shrimp Soup

Serves 4
Prep time: 10 minutes
Cooking time: 10 minutes

1 (14- to 16-ounce) can chicken broth or 2 bouillon cubes
    mixed with 2¾ cups water
½ cup water
2 tablespoons Thai fish sauce (naam pla) or soy sauce
1 tablespoon light brown sugar
1½ teaspoons ground ginger
¼ teaspoon salt
¼ teaspoon crushed red pepper flakes
2 ounces vermicelli or other thin pasta, broken
    into pieces
1¼ cups unsweetened coconut milk
3 scallions, thinly sliced
8 ounces canned, frozen, or fresh small shrimp, peeled,
    deveined, and halved widthwise
¼ cup chopped fresh cilantro
2 tablespoons fresh lime or lemon juice

In a large saucepan, combine broth, water, fish sauce, sugar, ginger, salt, and red pepper flakes. Bring to a boil, stir in vermicelli and cook until noodles are almost cooked through, about 4 minutes. Add coconut milk and scallions and bring to a simmer. Stir in shrimp and cook until just done, about 2 minutes. Stir in cilantro and lime juice and serve.

The ingredient list in this recipe may seem a little intimidating, but the soup is actually a breeze to make and has a great flavor payoff.

Be sure to buy unsweetened coconut milk. Use any leftovers in place of some of the water when cooking rice.

Look for Thai fish sauce in the imported foods section of larger supermarkets or Asian specialty stores.

TIPS

Lentil and Rice Soup

Filling and flavorful, this soup is almost a meal in a bowl.

Serves 6
Prep time: 15 minutes
Cooking time: 35 minutes

2 (14- to 16-ounces each) cans beef broth, or 2 beef bouillon
    cubes mixed with 3¾ cups water
2½ cups water
1 cup brown lentils, picked over and rinsed
¾ cup white rice
1 (32- to 28-ounce) can tomatoes, chopped with juice
2 carrots, chopped
1 onion, chopped
2 cloves garlic, minced
½ teaspoon dried basil
½ teaspoon dried oregano
1 bay leaf
¼ teaspoon ground red pepper, or a few drops hot red
    pepper sauce (optional)
2 tablespoons cider vinegar
4 ounces shredded Monterey Jack or cheddar cheese (1 cup)
Crumbled bacon or diced ham (optional)

In a large pan, combine broth, water, lentils, rice, tomatoes and juice, carrots, onion, garlic, basil, oregano, and
bay leaf. Bring to a boil, then reduce heat and simmer,
covered, stirring occasionally, for 45 minutes, or until
lentils and rice are tender. Stir in red pepper and vinegar.
Remove bay leaf. Top with cheese and bacon and serve.

Creamy Shrimp Bisque

Serves 4
Prep time: 5 minutes plus chilling
Cooking time: 10 minutes

1 (10½-ounce) can cream of shrimp soup, undiluted
1 cup whole milk
½ cup tomato juice
⅓ cup dry sherry

In a medium saucepan, whisk together soup, milk, and tomato juice. Bring to a boil, stirring, over medium heat. Add sherry. Reduce heat to low and simmer for 5 minutes. Serve hot or cold. To serve cold, refrigerate until chilled, at least 2 hours.

Serve this soup hot or make it in the morning and chill it for a late lunch. Serve with cucumber spears and crackers.

Peanut Butter Soup

Serves 4
Prep time: 10 minutes
Cooking time: 30 minutes

1 tablespoon olive oil
1 large onion, finely chopped
4 cloves garlic, minced, or 1 tablespoon garlic paste
1 stalk celery, halved lengthwise and thinly sliced
3 carrots, halved lengthwise and thinly sliced
⅔ cup creamy peanut butter
1 (14- to 16-ounce) can chicken broth, or 1 bouillon cube
    mixed with 1¾ cups water
2 cups water
1 teaspoon hot red pepper sauce
¾ teaspoon salt

Corn bread squares and crisp apples make good accompaniments to this soup.

In a large saucepan, heat oil over medium heat. Add the onion and garlic and cook, stirring frequently, for 10 minutes or until onion is golden. Add celery and carrots and cook until carrots are tender, about 4 minutes.

Stir in peanut butter until well combined. Add broth, water, hot pepper sauce, and salt. Bring to a boil. Reduce heat to low and simmer, covered, for 10 minutes. Serve.

Pasta and Bean Soup

Warm garlic bread makes an easy accompaniment to this Italian classic. If you have a jar of pesto on hand, swirl a little into each bowl, just before sprinkling on the cheese.

Serves 4
Prep time: 10 minutes
Cooking time: 25 minutes

2 tablespoons olive oil
1 large onion, finely chopped
3 cloves garlic, minced
3 cups water
1 (14- to 16-ounce) can Italian-style stewed tomatoes,
    chopped with juice
1 (14- to 16-ounce) can chicken broth
½ teaspoon dried rosemary, crumbled
½ teaspoon salt
½ teaspoon black pepper
1 cup small pasta shells
1 (15-ounce) can small white beans, rinsed and drained
⅓ cup grated Parmesan cheese

In a large saucepan, heat oil over medium heat. Add the onion and garlic and cook for 5 minutes, stirring. Add the water, tomatoes with juice, broth, rosemary, salt, and pepper.

Bring soup to a boil and add pasta shells. Reduce heat to low and simmer for 10 minutes. Add beans and cook, covered, for 5 minutes. Spoon soup into bowls, sprinkle with cheese, and serve.

Bean Soup with Tortillas

We've suggested some toppings here, but feel free to try others such as sour cream or chopped ham.

Serves 4
Prep time: 5 minutes
Cooking time: 15 minutes

1 tablespoon olive oil
1 large onion, finely chopped
3 cloves garlic, minced
1 tablespoon chili powder, or to taste
2 cups tomato or V-8 juice
2 cups water
2 tablespoons red wine vinegar
1 (15-ounce) can red kidney beans (not drained)

¾ cup prepared salsa
2 cups tortilla chips
4 ounces shredded Monterey jack cheese (1 cup)

In a large saucepan, heat oil over medium heat. Add onion and garlic. Cook, stirring, for 5 minutes or until onion is tender. Stir in chili powder. Cook for 1 minute.

Add tomato juice, water, vinegar, beans with liquid, and ½ cup salsa. Bring to a boil. Reduce the heat to low and simmer, covered, for 5 minutes. Divide chips among 4 bowls. Pour soup over chips and garnish cheese and remaining ¼ cup salsa.

Chilled Yogurt-Cucumber Soup

Serves 6
Prep time: 25 minutes plus chilling

3 cups plain low-fat or nonfat yogurt
1 cup water
½ cup half-and-half or milk
2 teaspoons Dijon-style mustard
3 scallions (including green tops), chopped
1 large seedless cucumber, peeled and chopped
1 cup finely shredded red cabbage (optional)
½ cup golden raisins (optional)
1 tablespoon granulated sugar
1 tablespoon chopped fresh dill, or 1 teaspoon dried dill
Dill sprigs for garnish

This soup makes a cool starter for grilled lamb or fish. It's also delicious for lunch with steak sandwiches. You can make it ahead as it refrigerates nicely.

In a large container, whisk together yogurt, water, milk, and mustard. In a bowl, combine scallions, cucumber, cabbage, and raisins. Sprinkle with sugar and dill and toss until coated. Add vegetables to yogurt mixture and stir. Cover and chill for 3 hours. Garnish with dill.

Chunky Gazpacho

This version of the ultimate warm weather soup can almost double as a salad. Turn it into a main course by adding peeled, boiled shrimp or crabmeat.

Serves 6
Prep time: 30 minutes plus chilling

3 cups V-8 juice (regular or spicy) or tomato juice
2 tablespoons extra-virgin olive oil
2 tablespoons fresh lemon juice
2 tablespoons balsamic vinegar
Worcestershire sauce to taste
6 large ripe tomatoes, seeded and chopped, or 3 (14- to
    16-ounces each) cans diced tomatoes, drained
2 seedless cucumbers, peeled and chopped
2 red, orange, or yellow bell peppers, seeded
    and chopped
2 garlic cloves, minced
⅓ cup finely chopped onion
2 tablespoons fresh basil, chopped, or 2 teaspoons
    dried basil
Salt and freshly ground black pepper to taste
Garlic croutons for garnish

In a large container, mix together the V-8 juice, olive oil, lemon juice, vinegar, and Worcestershire sauce. Add the chopped vegetables, basil, and salt and pepper. Cover and chill for at least 3 hours. Garnish soup with the croutons and serve.

Main Dishes

You've reached your destination. The lines are secured or the anchor is set. Now it's time to sit back and relax before dinner. Yes, even the cook will be able to relax. Using the recipes in this chapter, you can provide a fanciful feast to feed your hungry deckhands or special guests without too much work.

The key to making your evenings effortless is planning (and making) ahead. Marinated meats and poultry can be the keys to your success since they require minimal amounts of time and ingredients and net great flavor payoffs. You'll love serving the Grilled Chicken with Couscous and Pork or Beef Kebabs. For a special occasion try the Grilled Beef Tenderloin. Add some Herbed Potatoes (page 111) or the Provençal Potatoes (page 113) and a salad. Voila...you have a quick, easy and elegant meal.

The make-ahead dishes in this chapter, such as the Comfort Meatloaf, Pot Roast Plus, Homestyle Chicken Stew, and Shells with Little Meatballs, are great for that first night out on the boat. Just reheat and serve. What could be easier? The meatloaf, pot roast, and other recipes offer the added bonus of leftovers, which can be transformed in minutes into brand new dishes for the next day's lunch or supper (pages 68 and 69).

Pot Roast Plus

The ultimate comfort food! Bring it on board, and you've got culinary money in the bank—not only a great-tasting main dish, but the makings for sandwiches and a delicious pasta sauce.

Serves 6 with leftovers
Prep time: 35 minutes
Cooking time: 2½ hours

1 tablespoon olive oil
4 pounds boneless chuck roast
3 large onions, halved and thinly sliced
5 cloves garlic, slivered
3 carrots, peeled and thinly sliced
1 tablespoon granulated sugar
1¼ cups dry red wine or beef broth
1 (16-ounce) can crushed tomatoes
1¼ teaspoons salt
¾ teaspoon dried thyme, crumbled
¾ teaspoon black pepper
Grated zest of one small orange

Preheat oven to 350°F. In a Dutch oven or large pot, heat oil over medium heat. Add beef and cook until browned, about 5 minutes per side. Transfer meat to a plate.

Add onions and garlic to the pot and cook, stirring, for 10 minutes, or until onions are golden. Add carrots and sugar and cook, stirring, until onions are a rich brown color and carrots are tender, about 7 minutes longer.

Add wine and bring to a boil. Stir in tomatoes with juices, salt, thyme, pepper, and orange zest. Return to a boil and add beef. Cover and bake for 2½ hours, or until meat is tender. Remove meat from sauce. Skim any fat from sauce. Slice meat and serve immediately with the sauce, or slice and chill, covered, before transporting to boat. Reheat slices with sauce and vegetables in a large skillet over medium heat.

VARIATION

Leftovers also make a great pasta sauce. For 1 pound of pasta, use half of the meat, vegetables, and sauce. Coarsely chop meat and vegetables, then gently heat with half the sauce. Toss with cooked pasta (such as penne) and ½ cup grated Parmesan. Serves 4 to 6.

Grilled Beef Tenderloin

Serves 6 with leftovers
Prep time: 5 minutes plus marinating (optional)
Cooking time: 35 minutes

1 trimmed beef tenderloin filet (about 4 pounds)
2 tablespoons Cognac or red wine (optional)
¼ cup (½ stick) unsalted butter, softened, or
    2 tablespoons olive oil
Garlic powder to taste
Freshly ground black pepper to taste
Horseradish sauce (see TIP)

Rub filet with cognac and let stand for 30 minutes. Smear with butter to coat or brush with olive oil. Sprinkle with garlic powder and pepper.

Preheat gas grill to 450°F. or prepare charcoal grill.

If using a gas grill, bake filet for 10 minutes. If using a charcoal grill, place filet over very hot coals for about 10 minutes, turning once. Then, reduce heat to 350°F on gas grill, or move meat away from the coals and cover. Cook for about 25 minutes for medium-rare meat, or until internal temperature (using meat thermometer) is 135°F. (For rare meat, internal temperature should be about 125°F and for medium meat, it should be 145°F.) Check at 5 minute intervals.

Remove filet from the grill and let stand for 15 minutes before slicing. Cut into very thin slices on an angle. Serve with horseradish sauce (see TIP), if desired.

For only 5 minutes of preparation, you can have two elegant meals— the tenderloin fresh off the grill and a main-dish salad the next day (page 102).

For a simple horseradish sauce, combine 1 cup sour cream and ¼ cup prepared horseradish, drained. Season with salt and pepper to taste. Serve at room temperature or chill for 30 minutes.

T I P

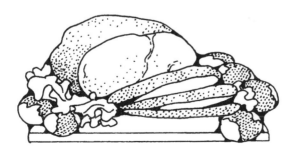

Pork or Beef Kebabs

Thanks to bottled salad dressing, this recipe is super easy. To make it even quicker, spray (see TIP) the vegetables with a vegetable oil cooking spray instead of brushing them.

Serves 4
Prep time: 15 minutes plus marinating
Cooking time: 15 minutes

1¼ pounds pork tenderloin or beef sirloin, cut into
    12 chunks
⅔ cup prepared honey-Dijon vinaigrette for pork or
    balsamic vinaigrette for beef
2 zucchini, each cut into 6 rounds
1 large red or green bell pepper, cored and cut into
    12 squares
1 medium red or yellow onion, cut into 8 wedges
    through root end
8 fresh mushrooms
3 tablespoons olive oil or vegetable oil

Place meat chunks and vinaigrette in a resealable plastic bag. Turn bag to coat meat evenly. Marinate, chilled, for 4 to 6 hours.

Preheat grill.

TIP

When using vegetable cooking spray on a boat, try to confine spraying to the sink to minimize spray cloud.

Brush the vegetables with the oil. Thread meat and vegetables on 4 long metal skewers, alternating 3 chunks of meat, 3 zucchini rounds, 3 pepper squares, 2 onion wedges and 2 mushrooms per skewer.

Grill the pork kebabs 12 minutes, turning once, or until cooked through. Grill the beef kebabs 10 minutes, turning once. Serve immediately.

VARIATIONS

Fruit can be added to the pork kebabs. For example, you can replace the mushrooms with large pineapple chunks.

If your package of pork tenderloin contains 2 tenderloins (about 1 pound each), just make more chunks for the kebabs, or grill the second tenderloin whole for about 15 minutes, turning once, and use it for sandwiches or in a stir-fry. Alternatively, freeze it at home, uncooked, for another use.

Comfort Meatloaf

Serves 6 with leftovers
Prep time: 15 minutes
Cooking time: 1 hour

2 pounds ground sirloin
1 pound ground turkey
½ cup chopped onion (fresh or frozen)
2 cups herb-stuffing mix, or 1 cup Italian-style breadcrumbs
1 tablespoon Worcestershire sauce
3 eggs, beaten
1½ cups prepared marinara sauce

Preheat oven to 350°F.

Combine sirloin, turkey, onion, stuffing mix, and Worcestershire sauce in a large bowl. Add eggs and 1 cup marinara sauce. Mix thoroughly. Place in a large meatloaf pan or shape into a loaf and place in a large, shallow baking dish. Spread remaining ½ cup marinara sauce over top of loaf.

Bake until cooked through, about 1 hour and 15 minutes. Let cool for 10 minutes, then cut into ¾-inch-thick slices. Wrap sliced loaf and chill until ready to transport. To serve, heat slices with the pan juices in a skillet over medium heat until heated through.

Serve this meatloaf for dinner one night, then use leftovers to fill hearty sandwiches (page 68) at lunch the next day. If you prefer, substitute salsa or ketchup for the marinara sauce.

Cincinnati Chili

The chili can be made ahead and frozen, then reheated at serving time. The pasta can also be made ahead then reheated as directed on page 42.

Serves 4 to 6
Prep time: 15 minutes
Cooking time: 30 minutes

2 tablespoons olive oil
2 medium onions, finely chopped
3 cloves garlic, minced
1½ pounds ground sirloin
2 tablespoons chili powder, or to taste
1½ teaspoons ground cinnamon
1 teaspoon ground cumin
1 teaspoon unsweetened cocoa powder
1 (28-ounce) can crushed tomatoes
2 teaspoons light or dark brown sugar
1 teaspoon salt
½ teaspoon black pepper
12 ounces spaghetti
4 ounces shredded cheddar cheese (about 1 cup)

In a large skillet, heat the oil over medium heat. Add the onions and garlic, and cook, stirring frequently for 10 minutes, or until the onion is golden brown and tender. Stir in the beef and cook, breaking up lumps with a spoon, for 3 minutes, or until no longer pink.

Stir in the chili powder, cinnamon, cumin, and cocoa powder and cook for 1 minute, or until meat is well coated. Stir in the tomatoes, sugar, salt, and pepper and bring to a boil. Reduce heat to low and simmer, covered, for 15 minutes, or until the sauce is flavorful. Cool, then refrigerate chili. Pack in a large resealable plastic bag or plastic container and refrigerate or freeze.

While chili is reheating, cook spaghetti according to package directions, then drain. Combine the drained spaghetti and chili and toss to mix. Serve with cheese sprinkled on top.

Shells with Little Meatballs

Serves 6
Prep time: 35 minutes
Cooking time: 40 minutes

MEATBALLS:
½ cup dry bread crumbs
¼ cup milk
1 pound ground sirloin
2 tablespoons chopped onion
1 tablespoon Worcestershire sauce
1 large egg
SHELLS:
8 ounces medium pasta shells, cooked according to
    package directions
1 (26-ounce) jar prepared tomato pasta sauce, or 3 cups
    canned herbed tomato sauce
½ cup diced sun-dried tomatoes (optional)
10 ounces shredded mozzarella cheese (about 2½ cups)
8 ounces grated Parmesan (or Asiago) cheese (about 1½ cups)
Additional shredded mozzarella to top casserole

This versatile recipe can be tailored to your travel schedule and cooking equipment. You can prepare the whole casserole at home and heat it up on the boat. For a longer trip, you can freeze the meatballs, then prepare the pasta and assemble underway. Heat it all up in the oven, on the stovetop, or in the microwave.

For meatballs: in a large bowl, combine breadcrumbs and milk and let stand for 5 minutes. Add meat, onion, Worcestershire sauce, and egg. Mix together gently and shape into small balls. Heat a large nonstick skillet over medium heat. Add meatballs and cook for 20 minutes, turning occasionally to brown evenly. Set aside.

Preheat oven to 350°F. Grease a 13 by 9-inch baking dish. Spread half the shells in prepared dish. Top with half the meatballs, 1 cup tomato sauce, ¼ cup sun-dried tomatoes, 1 cup mozzarella, and ¾ cup Parmesan. Repeat layers. Top with remaining tomato sauce and mozzarella. Bake for 20 minutes, or until bubbly. Let stand for 5 minutes before serving.

To cook on stovetop: Assemble as directed in a deep skillet. Cook over medium heat until bubbly.

To microwave: Assemble as directed in a microwave-safe dish. Microwave on medium for 6 minutes, or until bubbly.

Hearty Moussaka

With a moussaka in your freezer, you have a meal-in-one ready to pack up and take on the boat. If you like, you can round out the menu with a salad and garlic bread.

Serves 6
Prep time: 45 minutes
Baking time: 30 minutes (or 1 hour if frozen)

8 tablespoons olive oil
1 large onion, finely chopped
2 cloves garlic, minced
12 ounces ground lamb
1 (28-ounce) can crushed or diced tomatoes
1½ teaspoons grated orange zest
1½ teaspoons dried oregano, crumbled
2 teaspoons salt
½ teaspoon black pepper
¼ teaspoon ground allspice
1¼ pounds eggplant, thinly sliced
1 pound russet potatoes, peeled and thinly sliced
3 tablespoons all-purpose flour
3 cups milk
⅓ cup grated Parmesan cheese
6 ounces feta cheese, crumbled (about 1½ cups)

In a large skillet, heat 1 tablespoon of the oil over medium heat. Add the onion and garlic and cook for 7 minutes, stirring frequently, or until onion is tender. Add the lamb and cook, stirring frequently, for 3 minutes, or until no longer pink. Add the tomatoes, orange zest, 1 teaspoon oregano, 1 teaspoon salt, the pepper, and allspice. Bring to a boil, then reduce heat to low and simmer, covered, for 20 minutes.

Meanwhile, preheat the broiler. Brush the eggplant with 4 tablespoons of the remaining oil and sprinkle ½ teaspoon of the remaining salt over the eggplant. Place slices on baking sheet and broil 4 inches from the heat for 4 minutes per side, or until tender and soft. Set aside. In a large pot of boiling water, cook the potatoes for 5 minutes, or until tender but not falling apart. Drain well.

In a large, heavy saucepan, heat the remaining 3 tablespoons of oil over medium heat. Whisk in the flour and cook for 2 minutes, whisking, until well combined.

Gradually add the milk and cook, whisking, for 5 to 7 minutes or until the sauce is thick enough to coat the back of a spoon. Stir in the remaining salt, remaining oregano, and the Parmesan. If planning to serve now, preheat oven to 350°F.

Spoon one-third of the meat sauce into the bottom of an 11 by 7-inch glass baking dish. Top with half the potatoes, half the eggplant slices, and one-third of the white sauce. Sprinkle one-third of the feta over the white sauce. Spoon half the remaining meat sauce, all the remaining potatoes, and eggplant slices, half of the remaining white sauce, and half the remaining feta cheese on top. Finish with the remaining meat sauce, white sauce, and feta cheese.

To serve now: Bake for 30 minutes, or until piping hot and bubbly. To serve later: Chill casserole until cool. Wrap casserole in foil, label, and date. Freeze for up to 3 months. To serve: Preheat the oven to 350°F. Uncover dish and bake for 1 hour, or until bubbly.

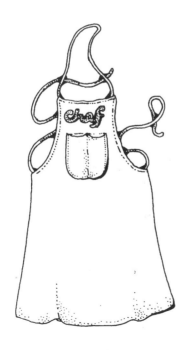

Taco Bake

This is a main dish for the whole family. With trash compacting in mind, we've called for boxed tomato sauce, but 3 cups of any tomato pasta sauce can be used. You can make the casserole at home up to the last step and freeze. Add the cheese and chip topping on board as directed.

Serves 4
Prep time: 20 minutes
Baking time: 35 minutes

½ tablespoon vegetable oil
1 pound ground beef or turkey
½ cup chopped onion
1 clove garlic, minced, or ⅛ teaspoon garlic powder
1 tablespoon chili powder
1 (7-ounce) bag tortilla chips
8 ounces shredded Monterey Jack/cheddar blend
    (about 2 cups)
1 (26.455-ounce) container Parmalat Pomi
    Marinara Sauce
Salsa for serving

Preheat oven to 350°F. Grease an 8-inch square or an 8½-inch round disposable foil baking pan.

Heat the oil in a large skillet over medium heat. Add the ground beef, onion, and garlic, and cook, breaking up the meat with a spoon, until meat is cooked through and onion is softened. Stir in the chili powder and mix thoroughly.

TIP

If chips in a 7-ounce bag aren't available, use half of a 13½-ounce bag.

Knead the chips in the bag to crush them slightly. In a small bowl, combine 1 cup chip pieces and ½ cup cheese. Set mixture aside.

Spread half the beef mixture in bottom of prepared pan. Top with about 2 cups chip pieces. Spread half the marinara sauce (1½ cups) over the chips. Sprinkle about 1 cup of the cheese over the sauce. Repeat layers with remaining beef, chips, sauce, and cheese.

Bake casserole for 25 minutes. Spread reserved chip and cheese mixture over top. Bake for 10 minutes longer, or until topping is lightly browned. Let stand for 5 minutes before serving. Serve salsa on the side.

Chicken Enchiladas

Serves 6
Prep time: 20 minutes
Baking time: 25 minutes

1 tablespoon olive oil
1 large onion, coarsely chopped
2 cloves garlic, minced
1 (28-ounce) can plum tomatoes
1 pickled jalapeño pepper
½ teaspoon salt
12 (7-inch) flour tortillas
2 cups shredded cooked chicken
1 cup canned corn kernels, drained,
    or frozen, thawed
12 ounces Monterey Jack cheese, shredded
    (about 3 cups)
1 (4½-ounce) can mild chopped green chilies
Shredded lettuce and diced tomato
    (optional)

The whole crew, regardless of age, will like this one-dish dinner. We've suggested a lettuce and tomato topping, but there are other options such as salsa, sour cream, chopped onion, olives, or avocado.

In a large skillet, heat the oil over medium heat. Add the onion and garlic and cook for 5 minutes, or until tender. Transfer to a food processor or blender; add the tomato, jalapeño pepper, and salt and blend until smooth.

Preheat the oven to 350°F. Spoon ½ cup of sauce into bottom of 13 by 9-inch baking dish. Dip both sides of each tortilla briefly in sauce. Scatter about 2½ table-spoons chicken and 1 tablespoon corn down the middle of each tortilla. Sprinkle half the cheese and all of the green chilies over the chicken and corn. Roll up tortillas.

Place tortillas as filled, seam-side down, in the baking dish. Spoon remaining sauce on top and sprinkle with remaining cheese. If desired, wrap and freeze casserole at this point. To serve, cover casserole with foil and bake at 350°F for 25 minutes, or until piping hot and bubbly. Scatter the lettuce and tomatoes over the tortillas just before serving.

Grilled Chicken with Couscous

You can make the marinade at home and transport it in an airtight plastic container.

Serves 6
Prep time: 15 minutes plus marinating
Cooking time: 20 minutes on the grill, 30 minutes in oven

MARINADE:
1 medium onion, thinly sliced
2 garlic cloves, minced
½ cup olive oil
Juice of 1½ lemons
1 tablespoon soy sauce
1 tablespoon dry Sherry or apple juice (optional)
1 tablespoon minced fresh ginger
1 tablespoon ground cumin
1 tablespoon chili powder
1 teaspoon turmeric
1 teaspoon dried oregano
½ teaspoon black pepper
CHICKEN:
6 boneless, skinless chicken breast halves
    (about 5 ounces each)
1 (5- to 7-ounce) box couscous
½ cup green olives, pitted and halved

In a bowl, combine marinade ingredients and mix well. Place chicken in a gallon-size resealable plastic bag. Pour in marinade. Seal the bag and shake to coat the chicken. Chill for 2 hours or up to 8, occasionally shaking bag.

Heat the grill to medium-high.

Remove chicken from the marinade. Reserve marinade. Pat chicken dry and place on grill rack. Grill, turning once, until cooked through, about 20 minutes.

While chicken is cooking, place the marinade in a small pan. Bring to a boil and boil for 5 minutes. Remove from heat and set aside.

Prepare couscous according to package directions. Stir olives into cooked couscous. Arrange the couscous on a platter. Top with the chicken and drizzle with reserved marinade.

VARIATION

To bake the chicken: Place it in a lightly greased baking dish. Bake at 350°F for 30 minutes, or until cooked through. Baste with pan juices occasionally during cooking.

Chicken Roll-Ups

Serves 4
Prep time: 15 minutes plus marinating
Cooking time: 15 minutes

1 pound thin-sliced chicken cutlets
¼ cup Herb-Garlic Vinaigrette (page 47) or other vinaigrette
1½ teaspoons fines herbes or other dried herb mixture
2 medium zucchini
2 medium red or green bell peppers
½ medium red onion
olive or vegetable oil
4 (10-inch) flour tortillas
8 tablespoons herbed cheese spread (such as Alouette)

Seal chicken, vinaigrette, and fines herbes in a resealable plastic bag. Gently knead bag to coat chicken thoroughly. Marinate, chilled, for at least 1 hour.

Slice zucchini lengthwise into 4 slices each. Cut peppers into thick strips (discard cores and seeds). Slice onion into 4 slices. Insert a toothpick horizontally into each slice to hold rings together. Brush vegetables with oil.

Preheat grill. Stack tortillas and wrap in foil.

Grill vegetables until cooked through and slightly charred, about 5 minutes per side. Grill chicken until cooked through. Cut vegetables and chicken into ½-inch strips. Remove toothpicks from onion slices and cut slices in half. Keep warm.

Warm wrapped tortillas on grill for 1 minute each side. Place each tortilla on a serving plate and spread with 2 tablespoons of the cheese. Place chicken and vegetables lengthwise off center on tortillas and roll up, completely enclosing filling. Serve immediately.

TIPS

Chicken can be marinated ahead and taken aboard in the plastic bag. Vegetables can also be taken aboard in a sealable plastic bag, already brushed with oil.

Avoid fat-free vinaigrettes in this recipe. The oil in the dressing keeps food from sticking to the grill.

Grilled Curried Chicken

Serves 6
Prep time: 15 minutes plus marinating
Cooking time: 25–35 minutes

MARINADE:
½ cup plain low-fat yogurt
½ cup vegetable oil
¼ cup lemon juice
1 small bunch of scallions, finely chopped, or ½ cup
    chopped onion
2 large cloves garlic, minced, or ½ teaspoon garlic powder
1 teaspoon curry powder
1 teaspoon chili powder
CHICKEN:
6 boneless, skinless chicken breast halves
    (about 6 ounces each)
1 (8-ounce) jar mango or apple chutney

In a small bowl, whisk together the marinade ingredients.
Reserve ½ cup of marinade for basting (refrigerate until
needed). Put chicken in a large sealable plastic bag and
add remaining marinade. Seal and turn to coat chicken.
Refrigerate for 2 to 4 hours, turning bag occasionally.

Prepare grill or preheat broiler.

Remove chicken from marinade and pat dry. Place
chicken on rack and grill or broil near heat source for
10 minutes, turning once. Move chicken away from heat
or reduce broiler to medium heat. Baste with reserved
marinade and grill or broil until cooked through, about
5 minutes longer. Serve with chutney on the side.

Homestyle Chicken Stew

Serves 4
Prep time: 15 minutes plus marinating
Cooking time: 50 minutes

1 pound boneless, skinless chicken breasts, cut into
    1-inch cubes
Salt to taste
Garlic pepper seasoning to taste
3 tablespoons unsalted butter or vegetable oil
1 cup whole baby carrots or 1-inch carrot chunks
1 cup cubed red-skinned potatoes
1 cup frozen pearl onions or chopped onion
1 large clove garlic, minced, or ½ teaspoon garlic powder
4 cups shredded green cabbage (about ½ medium head)
¾ cup sliced fresh mushrooms (optional)
½ teaspoon dried thyme
Pinch granulated sugar
1 (14- to 16-ounce) can chicken broth
1 cup dry white wine or chicken broth
1 tablespoon all-purpose flour
2 tablespoons chopped fresh parsley (optional)

Toss chicken with seasonings. Place in a sealable plastic bag. Refrigerate for up to 24 hours, or freeze. (Pack frozen into cooler for transport. Thaw before cooking.)

In a kettle, melt 2 tablespoons of butter over medium heat. Set remaining butter aside to soften. Add carrots, potatoes, onions, garlic, cabbage, and mushrooms to the kettle. Cook, stirring, for 5 minutes, or until cabbage begins to wilt. Stir in thyme and sugar.

Add broth and wine. Reduce the heat to low and simmer, covered, for 15 minutes. Stir in chicken, season with additional salt and garlic pepper seasoning, if desired. Simmer, covered, for 15 minutes, or until chicken is cooked through and vegetables are very tender.

Mix softened butter and flour into a paste. Stir into the stew, a little at a time, until sauce is slightly thickened. Stir in parsley and simmer for 1 minute longer. Serve.

Comforting and nutritious, this stew can be started at home and finished on board. It's delicious served over corn bread squares (page 128).

Asian Turkey Burgers

Take a break from regular burgers with this exotic variation. Serve with a salad of slightly sweetened cucumbers and carrots dressed with rice vinegar.

Serves 4
Prep time: 10 minutes
Cooking time: 10 minutes

1 pound ground turkey
2 tablespoons finely chopped scallions
2 tablespoons soy sauce (optional)
½ teaspoon five-spice powder
3 tablespoons vegetable oil
4 English muffins, hamburger buns, or Kaiser rolls, split
Plum sauce, sweet-and-sour sauce, or ketchup

Preheat grill.

In a large bowl, mix turkey, scallions, soy sauce, and five-spice powder gently but thoroughly. Shape into 4 patties. Brush patties lightly or spray with the oil.

Grill burgers for 4 minutes per side, or until cooked through. Grill muffin halves until lightly toasted. Serve burgers on muffins with the sauce of your choice.

T I P

Look for five-spice powder in the spice section or the ethnic foods section of large supermarkets.

Sausage Grits

You can substitute chicken breasts or shrimp for the sausage. For a breakfast treat, if you have leftover grits, spread them on a lightly greased pan and refrigerate. Cut chilled grits into squares or rounds and fry in butter and oil.

Serves 4
Prep time: 10 minutes
Cooking time: 15 minutes

1 tablespoon olive oil
1 pound Italian sausage, casings removed
3 scallions, thinly sliced
1 (14- to 16-ounce) can crushed or diced tomatoes
1½ cups milk
1½ cups water
¾ teaspoon salt
1 cup quick-cooking grits
6 ounces sharp cheddar cheese, shredded (1½ cups)
1 tablespoon unsalted butter
¼ teaspoon black pepper

In a large skillet, heat the oil over medium heat. Add the sausage and cook, stirring to break up pieces, until no pink color remains. Add the scallions and cook for 2 minutes. Reduce heat to low and stir in the tomatoes. Simmer for 10 minutes.

Meanwhile, in a large saucepan, bring milk, water, and salt to a boil over medium heat. Gradually add grits, then reduce heat to low, cover, and simmer, stirring, for 5 minutes or until the grits are tender and thick.

Remove from the heat and stir in the cheese, butter, and pepper, stirring until the cheese is melted. Divide grits among serving plates and top with the hot sausage mixture.

Main-Dish Fried Rice

Serves 4
Prep time: 25 minutes
Cooking time: 15 minutes

3 tablespoons vegetable or peanut oil
3 whole scallions, chopped, or 3 tablespoons chopped onion
2 large eggs, beaten
1 pound cooked chicken, cut into bite-size pieces
1 cup cubed ham
1 cup frozen peas (optional)
¾ cup cashew halves or peanuts, plus extra for garnish
3 cups cooked long-grain white rice
¼ cup soy sauce
¼ cup dry sherry (optional)
¼ cup canned chicken broth or chicken bouillon

The secret to great fried rice is starting with cold cooked rice. So if you're having plain rice for one meal, make extra for this recipe. Serve with additional soy sauce on the side.

In a large nonstick skillet, heat 1 tablespoon of oil over medium-low heat. Add scallions and cook, stirring, for 2 minutes. Stir in the eggs and cook until set. Transfer egg mixture to a plate and set aside.

Heat the remaining 2 tablespoons oil in the skillet. Add chicken, ham, peas, and ¾ cup of cashews. Stir-fry for 2 minutes. Add rice, soy sauce, sherry, and broth to skillet. Stir to coat. Fold in the egg mixture. Cover and cook for 2 minutes, or until heated through. Serve immediately, garnished with remaining cashews.

Savory Grilled Bluefish

The main course and a side dish are cooked in one package. Serve with rice to soak up the juices.

Serves 4
Prep time: 10 minutes
Cooking time: 25 minutes

1½ pounds bluefish filet
½ teaspoon salt
¼ teaspoon black pepper
1 medium fennel bulb
2 stalks celery, thinly sliced
1 medium tomato, seeded and diced
1 small onion, chopped
2 tablespoons olive oil
1 teaspoon dried thyme
1 navel orange, thinly sliced (unpeeled)

Prepare grill.

Place the fish on a sheet of heavy-duty foil large enough to enclose entire filet. Sprinkle with salt and pepper.

Remove the green tops from the fennel and trim bulb. Cut the bulb into thin slices. Layer fennel, celery, tomato, and onion on top of the fish. Sprinkle with oil and thyme. Place the orange slices over the vegetables.

Fold foil over filet and seal. Place packet on grill. Cook for 25 minutes. Carefully cut packet open and serve.

T I P
Take care when opening the foil packet. The steam will be very hot.

Mediterranean Tuna Steaks

For a great starter, serve gazpacho.

Serves 4
Prep time: 5 minutes
Cooking time: 10 minutes

4 fresh tuna or swordfish steaks, about 6 ounces
    each and ½ inch thick
2 tablespoons olive oil
Salt and black pepper to taste
4 tablespoons prepared olivada (olive paste) (see TIP)

Prepare a charcoal grill or preheat a gas grill to medium-high.

T I P
Olivada, an Italian olive spread, is a tasty addition to your pantry. Whisk it in salad dressing for extra flavor or toss it with hot pasta.

Brush the tuna steaks on both sides with the olive oil and sprinkle with salt and pepper.

Place tuna steaks on grill rack and grill for 3 minutes. Turn steaks and spread the cooked side of each steak with 1 tablespoon of the olivada. Continue grilling until just opaque in center, about 3 minutes longer.

Pirate's Pasta

Serves 4
Prep time: 30 minutes
Cooking time: 15 minutes

8 ounces penne pasta
3 tablespoons olive oil
2 large garlic cloves, minced
1 teaspoon dried oregano
1 teaspoon dried basil, or 1 tablespoon chopped fresh
½ teaspoon dried red pepper flakes (optional)
1 (28-ounce) can diced tomatoes, drained,
    with ½ cup liquid reserved
1½ pounds cooked diced chicken or medium shrimp,
    without tails
3 tablespoons sour cream (optional)
4 ounces feta cheese, crumbled (about 1 cup)
2 large scallions (including green tops), chopped,
    or 2 tablespoons freeze-dried chives
Freshly grated Parmesan or Romano cheese

You can make this tempting dish with chicken or shrimp. If it's available, use pesto-flavored rotini or rotini primavera in place of regular penne.

Cook pasta according to package directions.

Meanwhile, heat oil in a large nonstick skillet over medium heat. Add garlic, oregano, basil, pepper flakes, canned tomatoes, and reserved tomato liquid. Cook for 5 minutes. Add chicken or shrimp and cook for 2 minutes, or until heated through and shrimp are opaque. Add sour cream and stir until blended.

Drain pasta and add to skillet. Toss until combined. Sprinkle with feta and scallions and toss again. Serve immediately with grated Parmesan.

Vegetarian Lasagne

Serves 6 generously
Prep time: 40 minutes
Baking time: 25 minutes

12 lasagna noodles (12 ounces)
2 tablespoons olive oil
1 large onion, finely chopped
4 cloves garlic, minced
1 red bell pepper, cut into ½-inch chunks
2 medium zucchini, halved lengthwise and
     thinly sliced
2 medium yellow squash, halved and thinly sliced
¾ teaspoon salt
1 can (28-ounce) whole tomatoes, coarsely chopped
     with their juice
½ cup Gaeta or Kalamata olives, pitted and
     coarsely chopped
1 teaspoon dried tarragon
¼ cup chopped fresh parsley
1 (15-ounce) container part-skim ricotta cheese
½ cup grated Parmesan cheese
½ teaspoon freshly ground black pepper
12 ounces part-skim mozzarella cheese, shredded
     (about 3 cups)

In a large pot of boiling water, cook the pasta according to package directions; drain. Transfer pasta to a bowl of cold water to prevent sticking.

In a large skillet, heat oil over medium heat. Add the onion and garlic and cook, stirring, for 7 minutes, or until tender. Add bell pepper and cook for 5 minutes, or until tender. Add zucchini, yellow squash, and ¼ teaspoon of the salt and cook for 5 minutes, or until squash is tender. Stir in the tomatoes, olives, and tarragon and bring to a boil. Reduce heat to low and simmer, covered, for 7 minutes, or until sauce is slightly thickened. Remove from the heat. Stir in parsley and remaining ½ teaspoon salt.

Preheat the oven to 450°F. Lightly grease a 13 by 9-inch foil baking dish.

In a bowl, whisk the ricotta cheese until smooth. Stir in the Parmesan and the black pepper. Set mixture aside. In the prepared dish, spread ¼ cup of the vegetable sauce. Lay 3 noodles on top and spoon one-third of the remaining vegetable sauce over. Scatter ⅔ cup of the mozzarella over the sauce. Repeat the layers twice with the remaining noodles, sauce, and 1⅓ cups of the mozzarella cheese, ending with the noodles. Top the layers with the ricotta mixture.

Bake for 20 minutes. Sprinkle the remaining 1 cup mozzarella on top and bake for 5 minutes longer, or until the top is golden and cheese is bubbly. Let stand for about 10 minutes before serving.

To make ahead and freeze: Assemble and bake lasagne as directed for 20 minutes, but do not sprinkle with the 1 cup mozzarella. Cool completely, then wrap and freeze. To serve, thaw casserole and bake at 400°F for about 15 minutes. Sprinkle with the remaining mozzarella and bake for 5 minutes longer, or until top is golden and cheese is bubbly.

Barbecued Shrimp Kebabs

The barbecue sauce can be made at home and brought on board. It's also delicious on chicken, pork, or salmon.

Serves 6
Prep time: 20 minutes
Cooking time: 10 minutes

SAUCE:
1 (12-ounce) jar prepared chili sauce
½ cup orange juice
½ cup cider vinegar
½ cup firmly packed dark brown sugar
2 tablespoons soy sauce
1 tablespoon Dijon-style mustard
1 teaspoon hot red pepper sauce, or to taste
2 large cloves garlic, minced
KEBABS:
1½ pounds large shrimp, shelled and deveined
1 small red bell pepper, cut into 1-inch squares
1 small green bell pepper, cut into 1-inch squares
3 tablespoons vegetable oil

Prepare grill.

To make sauce, combine sauce ingredients in a medium saucepan. Bring to a simmer over medium-low heat and simmer for 5 minutes, stirring occasionally. Set aside 1 cup of sauce for serving.

Thread shrimp onto 6 metal skewers, alternating with bell pepper squares. Brush with the oil. Place skewers on grill about 6 inches from heat source. Brush with the barbecue sauce and cook for 3 minutes. Turn and brush with more sauce and cook for 3 minutes longer, or until shrimp are cooked through. Serve drizzled with reserved sauce.

VARIATION

To bake the shrimp, preheat oven to 400°F. Prepare the skewers as directed and place on a baking sheet. Brush with the oil, then with the sauce. Bake for 10 minutes, turning once, or until shrimp are just cooked through.

Salads & Side Dishes

Salads have become a multipurpose menu item. Gone are the days of only iceberg and Romaine. Now there are dozens of fresh greens and other vegetables that lend themselves to salads. Toss them with crumbled cheese and Herb-Garlic Vinaigrette (page 47) and you have a savory side dish; add slices of grilled chicken or beef for a filling entrée. Main dish salads make perfect boat food—they're a great way to use leftovers and there's no cooking required! Plus, many salads can also double as sandwich fillings.

If you're lucky enough to find a farmers' market on your cruise, be sure to stock up on a variety of fresh vegetables. They make a perfect snack as well as being boat-friendly since they require minimal cooking. You'll definitely want to try the easy-to-prepare Warm Chinese Broccoli Salad and the Carrot Salad with just a hint of pineapple that makes it a real kid favorite!

There's a passion for pastas in today's galleys. And for good reason! They store easily, have a long shelf life, are simple to make, and affordable. Whether tossed with oil, garlic, breadcrumbs and Parmesan (Pasta with Breadcrumbs) or mixed with tuna and chickpeas (Pasta with Chickpeas), pasta is certain to be a winner hot or cold.

Curried Chicken Salad

An easy way to dress up leftover chicken or turkey, this salad also doubles as a sandwich filling. Try it in pita pockets.

Serves 6
Prep time: 35 minutes plus chilling

1 cup mayonnaise
2 tablespoons canola oil
2 tablespoons curry powder
½ teaspoon dried red pepper flakes
6 ounces mango chutney
½ cup currants or golden raisins
½ cup chopped almonds, peanuts or cashews
3 cups shredded chicken or turkey
Leaf lettuce or red cabbage leaves for garnish

In a large plastic container, whisk together mayonnaise, oil, curry powder, and red pepper flakes. Stir in chutney, chopping any large pieces. Fold currants and nuts.

Add chicken and combine all. Cover and chill for 1 hour. Serve on a bed of leaf lettuce or shredded cabbage.

Tenderloin Salad

One bonus of grilling a tenderloin is this salad. For a simple, yet elegant lunch, accompany with bread and cheese. To save time, use a bottled balsamic dressing and add capers.

Serves 6
Prep time: 15 minutes plus marinating

DRESSING:
2 large shallots, chopped or 1 large clove garlic, minced
2 tablespoons Dijon-style mustard
2 tablespoons drained capers
2 teaspoons dried tarragon
¼ cup red wine or balsamic vinegar
¾ cup olive oil
SALAD:
1½ pounds leftover grilled beef tenderloin (page 81),
    sliced thin or in julienne strips
red leaf lettuce (optional)
9 cooked small red potatoes, quartered or 4 medium
    red potatoes
3 hard-cooked eggs, peeled and chopped
8 ounces grape or cherry tomatoes
½ small red onion, sliced thin

In a large bowl, whisk together the shallots, mustard, capers, and tarragon. Whisk in the vinegar, then slowly whisk in the oil until well mixed. Set aside ½ cup of dressing. Add the beef to dressing remaining in bowl and toss to coat. Marinate for at least 1 hour.

Remove meat from dressing. Arrange the lettuce on a platter. Place the meat in the center, surround with the potatoes, and garnish with the chopped eggs, grape tomatoes, and onion. Drizzle the remaining dressing over all. Serve immediately.

VARIATION
This salad is similar to the French classic, Salade Niçoise. If you don't want to use beef in the salad, substitute 1 (12-ounce) can of oil-packed tuna, drained, for the beef.

Salmon Salad

Serves 4
Prep Time: 15 minutes

¼ cup plain yogurt
2 tablespoons mayonnaise
2 tablespoons prepared horseradish, drained
1 (14.75-ounce) can salmon, drained and picked over
1 small cucumber, peeled, if desired, and diced
2 scallions (including some green tops), chopped (optional)

In a medium bowl, combine yogurt, mayonnaise, and horseradish. Stir until smooth. Add salmon, cucumber, and scallions. Chill if desired or serve.

Add some breadsticks or crackers alongside this salad for an almost instant lunch.

T I P

Cucumbers are often waxed to prolong shelf life. Waxed cucumbers should be peeled.

Roast Chicken Salad

This dressing makes a great dip for chips or crisp vegetables.

Serves 4–6
Prep time: 15 minutes
Cooking time: 5 minutes

DRESSING:
⅔ cup plain low-fat yogurt
¼ cup mayonnaise
¼ cup red wine vinegar
½ teaspoon salt
½ teaspoon black pepper
3 ounces blue cheese, crumbled
SALAD:
1 pound fresh green beans, trimmed
1 pint cherry tomatoes, halved
1½ pounds skinless, boneless roasted chicken,
    cut into bite-size pieces

TIP

To avoid dealing with chicken bones on the water, bone and cut chicken at home and bring it on board in an airtight plastic container, making sure it stays well chilled.

In a large bowl, whisk together the yogurt, mayonnaise, vinegar, salt, and pepper. Add the cheese and mix well.

In a pot of boiling water, cook the green beans 3 minutes, or until tender, then drain. Add to the bowl with the dressing along with the cherry tomatoes and toss well. Stir in the chicken, toss again and serve.

VARIATION
If you like, use bottled blue cheese dressing and a 15-ounce can of green beans, drained, in place of the fresh

Boat-Friendly Chef's Salad

We've called for salad greens but you can use cabbage or a combination of other shredded or chopped vegetables as a base.

Serves 4–6
Prep time: 10 minutes

5 cups mixed salad greens, washed, dried, and stored in a
    resealable plastic bag
4 ounces thickly sliced smoked turkey, cut into strips
4 ounces thickly sliced Virginia-style ham, cut into strips
4 ounces thickly sliced hard salami, cut into strips
1 cup halved cherry tomatoes
½ cup pitted black or green olives
2 hard-cooked eggs, quartered lengthwise

3 ounces cheddar, Swiss or havarti cheese, cut into bite size
   pieces or 3 ounces feta or blue cheese, crumbled
½ Vidalia or red onion, very thinly sliced (optional)
Salt to taste
Seasoned pepper mix to taste
Herb-Garlic Vinaigrette (page 47) or commercially prepared
   dressing of choice

Arrange greens in a large salad bowl. Arrange cold cuts
on top of greens. Sprinkle with cherry tomato halves and
olives. Arrange egg quarters around edge of salad and
spread cheese over all. Mound onion slices on top and
season well with salt and pepper mix.

To serve, drizzle with dressing and toss.

Apricot Chicken and Rice Salad

Serves 4–6
Prep time: 15 minutes

Sweet-and-sour flavors combine perfectly in this main dish salad. Try serving it with corn muffins and a cucumber salad.

DRESSING:
¼ cup frozen orange juice concentrate,
   thawed
¼ cup soy sauce
3 tablespoons Dijon-style mustard
3 tablespoons apricot jam
¼ cup vegetable oil
SALAD:
2 cups diced cooked chicken or turkey
1½ cups cooked white or brown rice
1½ cups chopped celery
4 scallions (including some green tops), chopped, or
   ¼ cup finely chopped red or yellow onion
½ cup slivered or sliced almonds, toasted if desired
   (see TIP)

In a large bowl, whisk together orange juice concentrate,
soy sauce, mustard, and jam. Whisk in the oil.

Add the chicken, rice, celery, and scallions and stir
to coat with the dressing. Just before serving, stir in
the almonds.

Toast almonds before leaving home. Spread almonds in a single layer in a shallow baking pan. Bake at 350°F until fragrant, stirring occasionally, about 10 minutes.

TIP

Tortilla Salad

When it's too hot to cook, this salad fits the bill for lunch or supper. You can marinate the beans at home and bring them on board in a large plastic container. Mix the rest of the salad in the container and sprinkle the chips on individual servings.

Serves 4–6
Prep time: 10 minutes plus marinating

⅓ cup olive oil
2 tablespoons fresh lime or lemon juice
1 garlic clove, minced
½ teaspoon ground cumin
¼ teaspoon salt
⅛ teaspoon ground black pepper
1 (15.5-ounce) can black beans
1 pound deli smoked or grilled turkey or
    chicken
2 tomatoes, diced, or 1 (15-ounce) can diced
    tomatoes, drained
1 (8- to 10-ounce) bag ready-to-eat salad greens,
    or 4 cups shredded cabbage or lettuce
1 (7-ounce) can corn or Mexicorn
4 ounces shredded Monterey Jack cheese
    (about 1 cup)
½ cup sliced celery
¼ cup chopped onion
3 tablespoons chopped fresh cilantro
    (optional)
1 cup bite-size tortilla chips (4 ounces)

In a large bowl, mix together the olive oil, lime juice, garlic, cumin, salt and pepper until blended. Rinse and drain the beans. Add to bowl and toss to coat with the dressing. Let marinate for 1 hour.

Cut the smoked turkey into ¼-inch wide slivers. Add the smoked turkey, tomatoes, lettuce, corn, cheese, celery, onion, and cilantro to the beans and toss to mix. Arrange chips around the edge of the bowl and serve.

VARIATIONS

For extra kick, a small can of diced chiles can be added. Instead of deli smoked turkey, leftover grilled chicken, turkey, or pork may be used. You'll need about 3 cups of slivers.

TIP

Carry the ingredients to the boat in individual plastic bags. Put salad together on board.

Pasta with Chickpeas

Serves 4–6
Prep time: 15 minutes plus marinating
Cooking time: 10 minutes

1 recipe Herb-Garlic Vinaigrette (page 47)
3 cups shredded red or green cabbage
2 carrots, shredded
1 small red onion, diced
2 celery stalks, with leaves
10 ounces (2½ cups) small bow ties,
    ditalini or other small pasta
1 (15-ounce) can chickpeas, rinsed
    and drained
½ teaspoon salt
2 hard-cooked eggs, coarsely chopped
    (optional)

This simple salad can stand on its own as a one-dish meal, or act as a colorful supporting player to a main course of grilled fish or chicken.

In a large bowl, combine the vinaigrette, cabbage, carrots, and red onion. Remove celery leaves, chop half of them, and reserve the remaining whole leaves. Halve the celery lengthwise and thinly slice, then add with chopped leaves to the bowl with the cabbage mixture. Marinate for 1 hour at room temperature.

In a large pot of boiling water, cook the pasta according to package directions, then drain well. Add the pasta, chickpeas, and salt to the bowl with the vegetables and toss to combine.

Serve salad warm or chilled topped with chopped eggs and garnished with reserved whole celery leaves.

VARIATION
For a heartier dish, add one 12-ounce can of tuna packed in oil to the bowl with the chickpeas.

Potato Salad with Smoked Oysters

This elegant but easy take on potato salad can be the centerpiece of a lazy lunch. Offer cheese, cucumber spears, and carrot sticks alongside.

Serves 4
Prep time: 15 minutes
Cooking time: 10 minutes

2 pounds small white or red new potatoes, quartered
⅓ cup olive oil
¼ cup red wine vinegar
1 tablespoon Dijon-style mustard
½ teaspoon salt
¼ teaspoon black pepper
2 stalks celery, halved lengthwise and thinly sliced
1 small red onion, finely chopped
1 red bell pepper, cut into ¼-inch dice
2 (3¾ ounces each) cans smoked oysters, drained
¼ cup chopped fresh parsley

In a large pot of boiling water, cook the potatoes until tender, about 10 minutes. Drain, reserving ¼ cup of the potato cooking liquid.

In a large bowl, whisk together the oil, vinegar, reserved cooking water, mustard, salt, and pepper. Add the hot potatoes, tossing gently to coat. Add the celery, onion, bell pepper, oysters, and parsley and toss to combine. Serve warm, at room temperature or chilled.

Bulgur and Lentil Salad

Bulgur, made from whole wheat berries, requires no cooking, just an hour's soaking and it's ready to eat. The small French lentils, if available, are delicious in this salad.

Serves 6
Prep time: 15 minutes plus chilling

SALAD:
1 cup coarse bulgur
1 cup hot water
1 cup canned lentils or red beans, drained
2 scallions, or 1 small onion, chopped
1 pint cherry or grape tomatoes, halved
DRESSING:
⅓ cup extra-virgin olive oil
3 tablespoons fresh lemon juice or red wine vinegar
1 teaspoon ground cumin
½ teaspoon dried oregano
Salt and pepper to taste

In a bowl, combine the bulgur and the water. Cover and chill for 1 hour, or until the bulgur is softened and water is absorbed.

Add lentils, scallions, and tomatoes to the bulgur. In a small bowl, whisk together dressing ingredients. Add to salad and stir to coat.

VARIATION

For a more substantial salad, top with 8 ounces crumbled feta cheese and ½ cup chopped Greek or other black olives.

Balsamic Beet Salad

Serves 6
Prep time: 15 minutes plus chilling

¼ cup balsamic vinegar
¼ cup orange juice
¼ cup olive or vegetable oil
1 red onion, thinly sliced
2 (15-ounce) cans sliced beets, drained
1 cup fresh orange sections or canned mandarin
    orange sections, drained

In a bowl, whisk together vinegar, orange juice, and oil. Add onion slices and toss to coat.

In a serving bowl, layer about one-third of the beets. Top with one-third each of the orange sections and onion. Repeat layers twice. Pour any remaining dressing over salad. Cover and chill for at least 1 hour.

If you like, top this salad with a little plain yogurt or sour cream before serving. Alternatively, serve with crackers or toasts spread with goat cheese or other creamy, soft cheese.

Warm Chinese Broccoli Salad

Sesame oil is available in two forms: dark and light. The dark oil has a much stronger flavor, so if you use it, you might want to adjust the amount called for here.

Serves 4–6
Prep time: 10 minutes
Cooking time: 5 minutes

1 large head of broccoli, cut into florets
4 ounces snow peas
2 tablespoons Oriental sesame oil (see Note)
2 tablespoons vegetable oil
2 large garlic cloves, minced
⅛ teaspoon crushed red pepper flakes
⅓ cup soy sauce
⅓ cup red wine vinegar
3 tablespoons honey or brown sugar
½ teaspoon ground ginger
1½ cups fresh bean sprouts (optional)

Blanch broccoli florets and snow peas in boiling water for 2 minutes. Drain.

In a large skillet, heat the sesame oil, vegetable oil, garlic, and red pepper over low heat for 3 minutes. Stir in the soy sauce, vinegar, honey, and ginger. Cook for 1 minute. Remove skillet from the heat and stir in the broccoli and snow peas. With a slotted spoon, transfer vegetables to serving plates. Top with the beans sprouts, if desired, and drizzle with some pan juices.

Carrot Salad

This healthful salad is nice to have on hand. Not only does it have kid appeal, it also keeps well. If you prefer, use the Maple Vinaigrette instead of yogurt.

Serves 4–6
Prep time: 10 minutes

4 large carrots, shredded (about 3 cups)
1 medium Vidalia or other sweet onion
½ cup of toasted walnuts or pecans
¼ cup golden raisins (optional)
¼ cup drained canned pineapple pieces (optional)
½ cup plain low-fat or nonfat yogurt
2 tablespoons fresh orange juice, or 1 tablespoon frozen
    orange juice concentrate, thawed

In a medium bowl, combine shredded carrots, onion, nuts, raisins, and pineapple. Whisk together yogurt and orange juice concentrate. Pour over carrot mixture and toss to coat. Serve or cover and chill thoroughly.

Maple Vinaigrette

Makes ¾ cup
Prep time: 5 minutes

1 small shallot or small yellow onion, minced
1½ tablespoons maple syrup or brown sugar
1½ tablespoons cider vinegar
2 teaspoons Dijon-style mustard
1 teaspoon Worcestershire sauce
½ cup vegetable oil

In a small bowl, combine shallot, syrup, vinegar, mustard, and Worcestershire sauce. Slowly whisk in the oil until vinaigrette is emulsified.

This sweet-and-sour dressing is delicious on a spinach or a carrot salad or in coleslaw.

Herbed Potatoes

Serves 4
Prep time: 5 minutes
Cooking time: 30 minutes

2 pounds small red-skinned potatoes
3 tablespoons olive oil
2 cloves garlic, crushed
1 teaspoon coarse salt
1 teaspoon dried rosemary
1 teaspoon dried thyme

Wash the potatoes and cut in half. In a medium nonstick skillet over low heat, combine potatoes and oil. Cook for 20 minutes on low, stirring occasionally to evenly brown the potatoes. Add the garlic, salt, rosemary, and thyme. Cover the skillet and continue to cook for 10 minutes longer. Serve immediately.

The great flavor of oven-roasted potatoes is duplicated here on the stove top. They are ideal with grilled steaks, but also delicious with grilled fish.

Spicy Spinach

The lively southwestern flavors of this dish complement simple main dishes such as grilled chicken or pork. If you have leftovers, reheat them and use as a dip with corn chips or raw vegetables.

Serves 4–6
Prep time: 10 minutes
Cooking time: 15 minutes

2 (10 ounces each) packages frozen chopped
    spinach, thawed
1 tablespoon olive oil
1 medium onion, finely chopped
3 cloves garlic, minced
3 tablespoons all-purpose flour
2¾ cups milk
1 teaspoon ground cumin
¾ teaspoon salt
1 pickled jalapeño, minced, or ½ teaspoon hot red
    pepper sauce
4 ounces Monterey Jack cheese, shredded (about 1 cup)

Place the spinach in a colander. Squeeze to extract as much liquid as possible. Set spinach aside.

In a medium saucepan, heat the oil over low heat. Add onion and garlic and cook for 5 minutes, stirring frequently, or until onion is tender. Stir in the flour and cook for 1 minute, or until well combined. Stir in milk, cumin, and salt and bring to a simmer.

Add spinach and jalapeño and cook for 5 minutes longer, or until spinach is tender and creamy. Stir in the cheese and cook, stirring, just until melted. Serve.

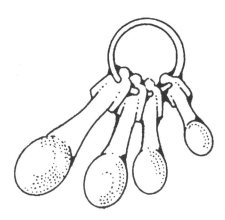

Provençal Potatoes

Serves 4–6
Prep time: 15 minutes
Baking time: 30 minutes

2 pounds red-skinned potatoes, scrubbed and cut into
    1-inch pieces
5 cloves garlic, peeled
1 teaspoon salt plus additional to taste
½ cup extra-virgin olive oil
½ teaspoon dried basil
½ teaspoon dried oregano
Ground black pepper to taste
2 medium-sized fresh or canned tomatoes, thinly sliced
    and drained
½ cup grated Parmesan cheese

Place potatoes and garlic in a large saucepan. Add water to cover and 1 teaspoon salt. Bring to a boil. Cook until potatoes are tender, about 10 minutes.

Preheat oven to 375°F. Lightly grease an 8-inch square disposable foil pan.

Drain the potatoes and garlic and return to pan. Add olive oil and, using a fork, coarsely mash potatoes with the garlic. Stir in the basil, oregano, pepper, and salt to taste.

Spoon half the potato mixture in a row along one edge of prepared pan. Place a row of tomato slices alongside, slightly overlapping the potatoes. Repeat rows. Sprinkle with the cheese.

Cover the pan with foil. Bake for 20 to 25 minutes, or until heated through. Remove foil and bake for 5 minutes longer, or until the cheese just begins to brown. Serve piping hot.

This savory side dish makes a great accompaniment to grilled steak.

Potatoes and garlic can be boiled at home and brought on board in a resealable plastic bag.

T
I
P

Pasta with Breadcrumbs

A classic Italian combination turns out to be perfect comfort food for boaters—and a great way to use up leftover bread. Serve with a tomato salad and pass extra cheese.

Serves 4
Prep time: 10 minutes
Cooking time: 10 minutes

12 ounces linguine or spaghetti
½ cup olive oil
6 cloves garlic, minced or crushed
¼ teaspoon crushed red pepper flakes
1 cup fresh Italian or French bread crumbs
¾ teaspoon dried oregano, crumbled
¾ teaspoon salt
½ cup grated Parmesan

Cook the pasta according to package directions; drain.

T I P

You can use stale bread for this recipe and make crumbs by grating the bread on a box grater. If the bread is still fairly fresh, you can cut it up into small pieces with a knife

Meanwhile, in a large skillet, heat the oil over low heat. Add garlic and red pepper flakes and cook for 2 minutes. Stir in breadcrumbs and oregano and cook 2 minutes, or until crumbs are lightly toasted. If the skillet is large enough, transfer drained pasta to it and add the salt and Parmesan. Otherwise, transfer the pasta, crumb mixture, salt, and Parmesan to a large bowl. Toss to coat, then serve.

Pasta Pancake

Leftover pasta works well in this recipe. The pancake may be served warm or at room temperature and is great for breakfast, lunch, or dinner.

Serves 4
Prep time: 10 minutes
Cooking time: 10 minutes

3 large eggs
½ cup grated Parmesan cheese
1 teaspoon salt
½ teaspoon black pepper
½ teaspoon dried oregano
3 tablespoons chopped fresh parsley or basil,
    or 2 teaspoons dried basil
4 cups cooked spaghetti (about 8 ounces
    uncooked)
1 tablespoon olive oil
3 tablespoons butter

In a large bowl, whisk together the eggs, Parmesan, salt, pepper, oregano, and parsley. Add the spaghetti and oil and stir to coat.

In a large (preferably nonstick) skillet, melt 2 tablespoons of the butter over medium heat. Add spaghetti mixture, pressing it gently to form an even pancake. Cook, without stirring, for 3 minutes, or until bottom is set. Then rotate skillet slightly so that the edge is closer to the burner (this will help the pancake cook evenly). Continue cooking and rotating the pan slightly until the bottom is golden brown and crisp. Gently lift the bottom of the pancake with a spatula to check to see how crisp it's getting. When the bottom is golden, carefully loosen pancake. Holding a heatproof plate or platter over the top of the skillet, invert the pancake onto the plate.

Add the remaining tablespoon of butter to the skillet and once it is melted, slip the pancake, golden side up, back into the pan. Cook 3 minutes longer, rotating the pan slightly as the pancake cooks, or until golden brown and crisp. Slide the pancake onto a serving platter. Serve warm or at room temperature.

VARIATION

For a heartier dish, add ½ cup of chopped ham to the egg mixture and proceed as directed.

If you like, make the pancake several hours or up to a day ahead and refrigerate. Bring to room temperature before serving.

T
I
P

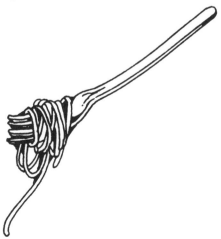

Noodle Stir-Fry

A variety of vegetables can be used in this stir-fry. It's a delicious way to use up the last carrot, a few broccoli florets, or steamed snow peas.

Serves 4–6
Prep time: 15 minutes
Cooking time: 10 minutes

4 tablespoons peanut or vegetable oil
2 large onions, halved and thinly sliced
4 cloves garlic, minced
3 tablespoons minced fresh ginger
2 red or green bell peppers, cut into julienne strips
3 cups shredded cabbage
3 cups cooked spaghetti (about 6 ounces uncooked)
3 cups shredded cooked chicken, ham, or pork
3 tablespoons firmly packed brown sugar
¼ cup soy sauce
¼ cup hoisin sauce or plum jam
1 tablespoon dark sesame oil
2 teaspoons cornstarch
¼ teaspoon salt
½ cup water

In a very large skillet, heat 2 tablespoons of the oil over medium heat. Add the onions, garlic, and ginger and cook for 5 minutes, stirring frequently, or until the onion is crisp-tender.

Add bell peppers and cabbage and cook for 5 minutes, stirring frequently, or until peppers are crisp-tender and cabbage is wilted. Add the spaghetti and chicken. Cook for 4 minutes, or until the spaghetti is heated through.

In a small bowl, whisk together the brown sugar, soy sauce, hoisin sauce, sesame oil, cornstarch, salt, and ½ cup of water. Stir the mixture into the skillet and bring to a boil, stirring. Cook for 1 minute, or until the vegetables and noodles are coated.

Breakfast

Rise and shine! Wipe your eyes, it's a new day. And what better way to begin the day than with new breakfast ideas? Scrumptious start-the-day-with-a-bang recipes are featured in this chapter.

Kids can be finicky at breakfast, but not with Toad-in-a-Hole. They'll love the name as well as the sandwich, in which eggs are cooked in a hole made in the toast—and it's so easy to prepare. Another quick kid-pleaser is the Tropical Fruit Sundae. Be sure to have plenty of the ingredients on hand—even your pickiest eaters will come back for seconds.

One thing you don't want to do is spend your morning in the galley. With that thought in mind, we've provided several recipes that can be made ahead and easily stored on your boat—Maple-Pecan Granola and Overnight Strata—as well as your own mixes for pancakes and corn bread. Are you drooling yet?

As you look over these recipes, think in terms of other times of day, too. Recipes such as the Captain's Corned Beef Hash, or either of the frittatas also make great supper fare. The Old-Fashioned Corn Bread can add a home-cooked touch to a meal of canned soup or stew. And the luscious cinnamon rolls are a delicious way of ending a meal as well as beginning the day.

Captain's Corned Beef Hash

With leftover potatoes and some deli corned beef, you can whip up a diner classic in a hurry.

Serves 4–6
Prep time: 15 minutes (more to boil potatoes)
Cooking time: 30 minutes

2 tablespoons butter
1 large onion, chopped
½ cup diced green or red bell pepper (optional)
1 teaspoon black pepper
1 pound finely chopped or shredded cooked corned beef or pot roast (page 80)
3 medium red-skinned potatoes, cooked and cut into small cubes
⅓ cup ketchup plus additional to taste

In a large skillet, melt butter over medium heat. Add the onion and bell pepper and cook, stirring, until onion is translucent, about 5 minutes. Stir in the black pepper.

Add the corned beef and potatoes. Cook for 20 minutes, turning hash with a spatula after 10 minutes, or until well browned. Stir in the ketchup and cook for 10 minutes longer. Serve hash with eggs (see note below) and extra ketchup.

Note: Poached eggs are the classic accompaniment to corned beef hash, but fried or scrambled eggs are equally delicious. To poach eggs, fill a small skillet with water and 1 tablespoon cider vinegar. Bring water to a simmer. Break an egg into a cup and slide it into the simmering water. Cook just under 3 minutes and carefully remove with a spatula or slotted spoon. Keep warm while you poach the remaining eggs in the same water. (You can poach two eggs at a time if the skillet is large enough.)

Overnight Strata

Serves 4
Prep time: 10 minutes plus chilling and standing
Baking time: 1 hour

8 ½-inch-thick slices of French bread (from a thin baguette)
4 ounces cooked ham, chopped
8 ounces shredded Swiss or extra-sharp cheddar
     cheese (about 2 cups)
2 teaspoons dried onion
3 large eggs
2 (12 ounces each) cans evaporated milk, shaken
2-3 teaspoons prepared mustard
¼ teaspoon black pepper

Grease an 8-inch square disposable foil pan.

Place 4 slices of the bread in one layer in prepared pan.
Spread the ham evenly over the bread, then spread the
cheese over the ham. Sprinkle dried onion over the
cheese. Place the remaining bread slices on top.

In a medium bowl, beat the eggs until well mixed. Stir in
the milk, mustard, and pepper until combined. Pour the
mixture over the bread, soaking every piece. Cover with
plastic wrap, and slide the filled dish into a gallon-size
resealable bag. Chill overnight. (NOTE: For food safety,
the refrigerator must be cold—below 40° F.)

Remove strata from refrigerator about 30 minutes before
baking. Preheat the oven to 350°F.

Bake strata for 45 minutes. Lay a sheet of foil lightly over
strata to keep it from over-browning, and bake for 15
minutes longer. Let the strata stand for about 5 minutes
before serving.

This strata is a great way to use up bread that is a little past its prime.

TIPS

Foil pans are great on a boat—no cleanup and no soaking or scrubbing. They also fit into resealable plastic bags.

In place of evaporated milk, you can use 3 cups of Parmalat milk, which is handy to have on board in any case. Parmalat containers collapse when empty, creating less garbage to stow or recycle.

Toad-in-a-Hole Breakfast

This recipe serves 4, but you can increase or decrease the number of servings by adding or subtracting eggs and slices of cheese, ham, and bread. For a sumptuous breakfast feast, serve with melon wedges.

Serves 4
Prep time: 5 minutes
Cooking time: 6 minutes

4 slices whole-grain bread
3 tablespoons butter
4 large eggs
4 slices deli ham
4 slices cheese (Swiss, Cooper sharp, jack or cheddar)
Salt and pepper to taste

Place bread on a cutting board. Use a drinking glass to cut out a round hole in the center of each piece of bread. Set aside rounds.

Melt 1 tablespoon of butter in a large skillet over medium heat. Place 2 pieces of bread in the skillet with the butter. Break an egg into each hole. Cover and cook for 3 minutes (the bread can be flipped if desired). Top each slice of bread with a slice of ham and and a slice of cheese. Cover and cook 1 minute longer. Use a spatula to transfer the toads-in-a-hole to a platter or baking sheet and keep warm. Repeat with remaining eggs, bread, ham, cheese, and 1 tablespoon of remaining butter.

After all are cooked, melt the remaining tablespoon of butter in the skillet and brown the 4 reserved bread rounds on both sides. Top each toad-in-a-hole with a toasted round and serve.

Breakfast Burrito

Serves 4
Prep time: 5 minutes
Cooking time: 15 minutes

8 slices Oscar Mayer or other brand precooked bacon
  (see TIP)
1 (14.5-ounce) can sliced new potatoes, drained, rinsed,
  and patted dry or 1½ cups leftover cooked potatoes
¼ cup chopped onion
4 (10-inch) flour tortillas
8 large eggs
½ cup shredded cheddar cheese
Salsa or ketchup (optional)

In a large skillet over medium heat, fry precooked bacon slices until crisp. Set slices aside. Fry potatoes and onions in fat remaining in skillet, breaking up slices with a spatula, until slightly browned and crisp. (Add a little butter if there is too little bacon fat.)

Wrap tortillas in foil and warm, either in the oven or over a burner.

Break up bacon into coarse pieces. In a bowl, beat eggs until blended. Add the bacon and eggs to potato mixture in skillet and cook, stirring, until eggs are firm.

Place a quarter of the egg mixture on each tortilla, sprinkle 2 tablespoons of cheese over each serving of egg, fold up bottom edge of tortillas, and roll into burritos. Serve immediately with salsa or ketchup, if desired.

VARIATION

Defrosted frozen hash brown patties can be used instead of canned potatoes. Break them up while heating in the skillet, before adding eggs and bacon.

TIPS

Precooked packaged bacon is great for boats. There's very little bacon grease to deal with. Furthermore, you get 14 slices in a package, which is almost the equivalent of a pound of uncooked.

Two containers of frozen egg substitute, defrosted, can be used in place of the 8 whole eggs.

Pesto-Prosciutto Frittata

For the kids, you can call this recipe green eggs and ham!

Serves 4
Prep time: 5 minutes
Cooking time: 20 minutes

6 large eggs
2 ounces prosciutto, cut into slivers, or
    ½ cup chopped ham
2 tablespoons prepared pesto
¼ teaspoon black pepper
1 tablespoon butter

Beat together eggs, prosciutto, pesto, and pepper. Melt butter in an 8 to 10-inch nonstick skillet over medium-low heat. Pour egg mixture into skillet. Cook for 15 minutes, without stirring, or until set and almost cooked through. Slide eggs onto a plate, invert skillet over plate, and flip, so uncooked side of frittata is on bottom in skillet. Cook for 2 minutes longer, or until cooked through. Cut into wedges and serve hot or warm.

Parmesan-Potato Frittata

Serves 6
Prep time: 10 minutes
Cooking time: 35 minutes

2 tablespoons olive oil
1 large onion, finely chopped
2 cloves garlic, minced
½ teaspoon salt
2 medium potatoes, or 1 large russet potato, cooked,
    peeled and thinly sliced
8 large eggs
½ cup grated Parmesan cheese
½ teaspoon rubbed sage or oregano
¼ teaspoon black pepper

In a large nonstick skillet, heat 1 tablespoon of the oil over medium-low heat. Add onion and cook, stirring, for 10 minutes, or until golden brown. Add garlic and ¼ teaspoon salt and cook, stirring, for 3 minutes longer.

Add potatoes and toss to mix. Transfer mixture to a plate and cool to room temperature. Wipe out skillet and set aside.

In a large bowl, beat eggs, remaining ¼ teaspoon salt, the cheese, sage, and pepper. Stir in the potato mixture. Add remaining 1 tablespoon of oil to reserved skillet and heat over medium-low heat. Pour egg mixture into skillet. Cook over low heat until frittata is set, about 25 minutes. Let cool slightly and cut into wedges and serve.

(If desired, you can place frittata under the broiler for 2–3 minutes to brown it.)

Grilled Ham Steaks with Orange-Honey Glaze

Serves 4
Prep time: 5 minutes
Cooking time: 5 minutes

3 tablespoons orange marmalade
3 tablespoons honey or maple syrup
1 tablespoon flavorful rum such as Mount Gay
4 ½-inch-thick, fully cooked ham steaks or sliced
    Canadian bacon

Prepare grill.

In a small bowl, stir together the marmalade, honey, and rum. Brush glaze over one side of ham steaks. Grill steaks for 1½ minutes on brushed side, brushing more glaze on the other side. Turn steaks and grill 1½ minutes longer. Repeat brushing and grilling, so both sides have been brushed and grilled twice, about 3 minutes total per side. Serve any remaining glaze on the side.

To cook on stovetop: Combine marmalade, honey, and rum in a large skillet and stir to mix well. Add the ham steaks and cook over medium heat until heated through, turning once.

What could be better than sizzling ham, hot off the grill? Serve with pancakes or French toast.

Consider buying individually cryovaced ham steaks, which are easy to take and keep on a boat.

**T
I
P**

Maple-Pecan Granola

Make up a batch of this hearty cereal at home and keep it handy, not only for breakfast, but for snacking.

Serves 6
Prep time: 6 minutes
Cooking time: 40 minutes

3 cups rolled oats
1½ cups pecans, coarsely chopped
½ cup maple syrup
3 tablespoons vegetable oil
3 tablespoons brown sugar
¼ teaspoon salt
1½ teaspoons vanilla extract
¾ cup dried cherries, raisins, currants, or dried cranberries

Preheat oven to 300°F. Lightly oil a 13 by 9-inch baking pan. Combine oats and pecans in prepared pan and toast until oats are fragrant, about 20 minutes.

Meanwhile, in a small saucepan, combine syrup, oil, sugar, and salt. Bring to a boil over medium heat. Remove from heat and stir in vanilla.

Increase oven temperature to 350°F. Pour syrup mixture over oat mixture and toss until combined well. Bake until granola is golden and crisp, about 15 minutes. Remove from oven, add cherries, and stir to combine. Cool granola, then break up any clumps. Store in an airtight container.

Tropical Fruit Sundaes

Feel free to alter the combination of fruits to suit your own tastes. Some that work well are cantaloupe, bananas, grapes, and mandarin oranges.

Serves 4
Prep time: 15 minutes

1 mango, peeled and cut into chunks
1 (16-ounce) container low-fat or nonfat vanilla yogurt
1 cup maple-pecan granola (see recipe above)
1 can (20-ounce) pineapple chunks packed in juice, drained
2 black plums, halved, pitted and cut into ½-inch
    thick wedges

Divide mango chunks among 4 bowls. Top with 2 tablespoons of yogurt and 1 tablespoon of granola. Using half the pineapple, spoon a layer of pineapple chunks on top, then add 2 tablespoons of yogurt and 1 tablespoon of granola. Top with all of the plums, 2 tablespoons of yogurt, and 1 tablespoon of granola. Repeat layers of pineapple, yogurt, and granola and serve.

Ham and Cheese Scones

Makes 8 scones
Prep time: 10 minutes
Baking time: 15 minutes

2 cups commercial biscuit mix, plus more for kneading
¾ cup shredded cheddar cheese
½ cup chopped Virginia-style smoked ham
¼ cup milk
3 tablespoons butter, melted
1 large egg

Preheat oven to 400°F.

Stir together biscuit mix, cheese, and ham in a large bowl. In a cup, beat together milk, butter, and egg.

Stir milk mixture into biscuit mix until a medium dough forms. Turn dough out onto a surface that is generously sprinkled with biscuit mix. Knead dough lightly 6 to 8 times, then form into a ball. Press or roll into a 9-inch round and transfer to an ungreased baking sheet. Cut the round almost through into 8 wedges.

Bake scones for 15 minutes, or until puffed and golden brown. Cool for 10 minutes, then break into wedges. Serve hot or warm.

Serve the scones with marmalade or warm apple sauce.

Buttermilk Pancakes

Everyone loves pancakes. In addition to maple syrup, you could offer fruit yogurt or leftover Citrus-Spiced Fruit (page 134) as a topping.

Makes 8 (4-inch) pancakes
Prep time: 5 minutes
Cooking time: 10 minutes

1¾ cups Pancake Mix (page 48)
1 large egg
¾ cup water or milk
½ teaspoon vanilla extract, optional

In a bowl, stir together pancake mix, egg, water, and vanilla. Stir in additional water if batter is too thick.

Preheat and lightly grease a frying pan or griddle. For each pancake, pour about ¼ cup of batter onto hot pan. Cook until bubbles begin to form on top and edges start to look dry. Using a spatula, turn pancakes and cook for 45 seconds longer, or until browned. Serve immediately.

VARIATIONS

When making the batter, stir in fresh fruit, such as cut-up bananas or blueberries. You can also add cooked and chopped bacon or ham or chopped nuts and raisins.

Cinnamon Rolls

Makes 12 rolls
Prep time: 10 minutes
Baking time: 15 minutes

1 (12-ounce) package refrigerator biscuit dough
3 tablespoons butter, melted
3 tablespoons granulated sugar
¾ teaspoon ground cinnamon
⅓ cup chopped pecans
⅓ cup currants or raisins

Preheat the oven to 400°F. Grease a baking sheet or two 8-inch square disposable foil pans.

On a lightly floured surface, roll biscuit dough out to a 12 by 5-inch rectangle. Brush dough with melted butter.

In a small bowl, stir together the sugar and cinnamon. Sprinkle the cinnamon sugar over the dough. Scatter the nuts and currants over the cinnamon sugar.

Starting from a long end, roll the dough up jellyroll fashion to a 12-inch-long roll. Slice into twelve 1-inch slices. Place the rolls on prepared baking sheet or pans.

Bake for 12 minutes, or until puffed and crisp. Let rolls cool for 10 minutes. Serve warm.

VARIATIONS

If you happen to have the ingredients on board, it's easy to whip up a glaze for the rolls. In a small bowl, stir together 1 cup of confectioners' sugar and 2 tablespoons milk or orange juice until smooth. Use a fork to drizzle the glaze over the warm rolls.

Old-Fashioned Corn Bread

Corn bread is not only great for breakfast, it's also good with other dishes such as chili, beef or chicken stew, or soups.

Serves 6
Prep time: 5 minutes
Baking time: 25 minutes

1 recipe Corn Bread Mix (page 48)
1 large egg
¼ cup vegetable oil
1¼ cups water

Preheat oven to 400°F. Lightly grease an 8-inch square baking pan or disposable foil pan.

In a bowl, combine corn bread mix with egg, oil, and water. Stir until well mixed. Pour into prepared pan. Bake for 25 minutes, or until firm on top and edges just start to brown.

VARIATION

Cheddar-Apple Corn Bread Wedges
Grease an 8½-inch round foil pan instead of square pan. Prepare batter as directed, but stir in 1 cup shredded extra sharp cheddar cheese. Core and cut one Golden Delicious or other cooking apple into about 10 wedges. Place apple wedges, skin side up, in a sunburst pattern in the corn bread mixture, pushing wedges in slightly. Bake as directed above. Serve hot, warm, or at room temperature, cut into wedges.

TIP

Carry corn bread mix in a heavy-duty sealable plastic bag. Then just add egg, oil, and water to bag. Reseal and gently squeeze bag to combine the ingredients.

Desserts & Beverages

Good desserts are always in demand. But many dessert recipes just don't lend themselves to boating. They're either too time consuming to make, too delicate for those pounding waves, or they require freezing—a luxury that is not available on many recreational boats.

Many of the recipes in this chapter can be made ahead and stored in resealable plastic bags or airtight containers. You can serve them with little fuss at the end of a meal or as an afternoon pick-me-up. If chocolate is a family favorite, try making the Cherry-Chocolate Brownies, the Everything Cookies, or the Chocolate Marshmallow Crème Fudge. Or, if you need something spur of the moment, your crew will love the Orange Pudding or the Easy Raspberry Trifle.

Being out on the water in the hot sun always brings on a thirst. Rather than serving the usual bottled or canned beverages, why not surprise your gang with Guava Punch or Cranberry Pink Lemonade? And if it's adults-only, try the Rum Punch made with guava juice. You'll think you're cruising the Caribbean!

Cherry-Chocolate Brownies

Everything Cookies

Pound Cake

Banana-Walnut Cake

Citrus-Spiced Fruit

Warm Sautéed Bananas

Orange Pudding

Apple Crisp

Chocolate Marshmallow Crème Fudge

Chocolate Date-Nut Bars

Easy Raspberry Trifle

Iced Mocha

Cranberry Pink Lemonade

Guava Punch

Rum Punch

Cherry-Chocolate Brownies

Tart-sweet dried cherries make these fudgy squares special. Pack up a tin and bring it along for a luxurious instant dessert. Buy extra cherries and use them to sprinkle on oatmeal or in trail mix or granola.

Makes 24 bars
Prep time: 20 minutes
Baking time: 30 minutes

4 (1 ounce each) squares unsweetened chocolate
2 cups granulated sugar
1 cup (2 sticks) unsalted butter, softened
4 eggs
1½ teaspoons vanilla extract
1 cup all-purpose flour
¼ teaspoon salt
½ cup coarsely chopped dried cherries
½ cup coarsely chopped pecans

Preheat the oven to 325°F. Lightly grease a 13 by 9-inch pan.

In a small heavy saucepan, melt chocolate over low heat. Set aside.

In a large bowl with an electric mixer, beat together sugar and butter until fluffy. Add eggs and beat until well blended. Stir in melted chocolate and vanilla. With mixer on low speed, beat in flour and salt. Fold in cherries and pecans. Pour batter into prepared pan.

Bake for 30 minutes, or until just set. Let cool in pan for about 20 minutes before cutting into squares.

T I P **If cherries are too dry, soak them in hot water for 15 minutes before chopping.**

Everything Cookies

Makes about 36 cookies
Prep time: 15 minutes
Baking time: 10 minutes per batch

1½ cups all-purpose flour
1 teaspoon baking soda
½ teaspoon salt
½ teaspoon ground cinnamon
1 cup (2 sticks) unsalted butter, softened
1 cup packed light brown sugar
½ cup granulated sugar
2 eggs
1 teaspoon vanilla
2 cups old-fashioned rolled oats
1 cup coarsely chopped walnuts or sliced almonds
1 cup semi-sweet chocolate chips
1 cup raisins

Preheat oven to 350°F.

Sift together flour, baking soda, salt, and cinnamon. Set aside.

In a large bowl with an electric mixer, beat butter, brown sugar, and granulated sugar until well combined. Add eggs and beat well. Stir in flour mixture just until mixed. Stir in vanilla and oats. Fold in nuts, chocolate chips, and raisins. Drop dough by generous teaspoonfuls about 2 inches apart onto ungreased baking sheets.

Bake in batches until firm and edges are just golden, about 12 minutes. Cool cookies on baking sheets for 2 minutes, then transfer with a spatula to a wire rack to cool. Store in an airtight container.

VARIATIONS

There are many possible additions to these cookies:
Instead of raisins, try dried cranberries or diced dried apricots.
In place of semi-sweet chocolate chips, try butterscotch or white chocolate chips.
For a sophisticated flavor twist, add 1 teaspoon grated orange zest to the dough with the vanilla.

These crunchy morsels will satisfy cookie fans of both persuasions— oatmeal and chocolate chip. They freeze well too, so you might want to make up a couple of batches at home and keep extras on board or for at-home snacking.

Pound Cake

Easy to eat and serve, this old-fashioned classic is as versatile as it is delicious. It makes a great accompaniment to fresh fruit or a fruit compote, or brush slices with a little butter and toast them for a decadent breakfast treat.

Makes two 8 by 4-inch loaf cakes
Prep time: 25 minutes
Baking time: 1 hour

3 cups all-purpose flour
¼ teaspoon salt
1 cup (2 sticks) unsalted butter, softened
3 cups granulated sugar
5 eggs
¼ teaspoon baking soda
1 tablespoon hot water
1 cup buttermilk or plain low-fat yogurt
2 teaspoons vanilla extract

Preheat oven to 300°F. Grease two 8 by 4-inch loaf pans. On a sheet of waxed paper, sift together flour and salt.

Place butter in a large bowl. Beat with an electric mixer on medium speed until smooth. Gradually add sugar, beating until fluffy. Add eggs, one at a time, beating for about 1 minute after each addition.

In a small bowl or cup, dissolve baking soda in the hot water. Add 1 cup of flour mixture to batter and beat until just combined. Beat in half of the buttermilk and the baking soda mixture. Add 1 cup remaining flour mixture, beating until just combined. Beat in remaining buttermilk and the vanilla, then beat in remaining flour.

Scrape batter into prepared pans. Bake until just springy to the touch, about 45 minutes. Cool on a wire rack for about 15 minutes, then turn out of pans and cool completely. Store in an airtight container or wrap well and freeze.

VARIATIONS

Change the flavor of the cake by adding ¼ teaspoon almond extract or 1 teaspoon grated lemon or orange zest. Or add a glaze.

Banana-Walnut Cake

Makes an 8-inch square cake
Prep time: 20 minutes
Baking time: 1 hour

STREUSEL:
½ cup all-purpose flour
¼ cup packed light brown sugar
½ teaspoon ground cinnamon
¼ cup (½ stick) butter, softened
⅓ cup chopped walnuts
CAKE:
1 cup granulated sugar
½ cup (1 stick) butter, softened
2 eggs
1 cup mashed ripe bananas (about 2 medium)
¼ cup milk
1 tablespoon baking powder
1 teaspoon vanilla extract
½ teaspoon ground cinnamon
⅛ teaspoon ground nutmeg
½ teaspoon salt
2 cups all-purpose flour
½ cup chopped walnuts

This moist cake makes a delicious accompaniment to coffee, morning or evening.

Cake may be made in a 9-inch square pan. Reduce baking time to 55 minutes.

TIP

For the streusel: In a medium bowl, stir together flour, brown sugar, and cinnamon. Stir in butter until mixture is crumbly, then fold in nuts. Set aside.

For the cake: Preheat oven to 350°F. Grease an 8-inch square baking pan or disposable foil pan.

In a large bowl using an electric mixer, beat granulated sugar and butter until creamy. Add eggs, one at a time, beating well after each addition. Beat in bananas, milk, baking powder, vanilla, cinnamon, nutmeg, and salt. (Mixture may look curdled.) On low speed, beat in flour, then fold in walnuts. Spread batter into prepared pan. Sprinkle the streusel over batter.

Bake for 1 hour, or until cake tester inserted into center comes out with a few moist crumbs. Place pan on a wire rack to cool completely.

Citrus-Spiced Fruit

Lemon and vanilla combine to dress up summer fruits. Serve over pound cake or topped with a little vanilla yogurt.

Serves 4
Prep time: 15 minutes plus cooling if desired
Cooking time: 10 minutes

1 teaspoon grated lemon zest
½ cup fresh lemon juice
½ cup granulated sugar
⅓ cup water
1 vanilla bean, split lengthwise, or 1 teaspoon vanilla extract
½ teaspoon ground ginger
2 firm ripe peaches, halved, pitted, and cut into 1-inch chunks (2 cups)
3 firm, ripe black or red plums, halved, pitted, and cut into 1-inch chunks (1½ cups)
2 large bananas, peeled and cut into 1-inch pieces

In a medium saucepan, stir together lemon zest, lemon juice, sugar, water, vanilla bean (not extract), and ginger. Bring to a boil over medium heat. Reduce heat to low. Add peaches and plums and simmer until tender, about 7 minutes. (Timing will vary depending upon ripeness of the fruit.)

Add the bananas and cook for 1 minute longer. If using vanilla extract, add it now. Remove the vanilla bean and with a small paring knife, scrape the seeds into the liquid before serving.

Serve fruit warm or transfer to a bowl, cool to room temperature, then refrigerate until chilled, about 2 hours, or up to 2 days.

VARIATION

If fresh fruit is not available, substitute 2 cans (15 or 16 ounces each) of water-packed sliced peaches or pears, drained, for the fresh peaches and plums. Chill fruit in syrup after cooking to help it absorb the flavors.

Warm Sautéed Bananas

Serves 4
Prep time: 5 minutes
Baking time: 10 minutes

2 tablespoons butter
½ cup apricot preserves
1½ tablespoons lemon juice
⅓ cup light rum (optional)
2 teaspoons vanilla extract
3 large ripe bananas
Ground cinnamon for garnish

In a large skillet, melt butter and preserves over low heat, stirring. Slowly stir in lemon juice and rum. Simmer for 2 minutes. Remove skillet from heat and stir in vanilla.

Peel bananas and cut into 6 or 8 pieces. Add to skillet. Cook over low heat, spooning sauce over bananas and turning them occasionally, until heated through. Serve sprinkled with cinnamon.

Rich, luscious, and quick—serve this almost instant dessert with a dollop of sour cream or yogurt sweetened with a little brown sugar.

Orange Pudding

Serves 6
Prep time: 10 minutes plus chilling

2 (11 ounces each) cans mandarin oranges
Orange juice, if necessary
2 packages vanilla instant pudding
1 (8-ounce) container vanilla yogurt

Drain mandarin oranges, reserving juice. To the reserved juice, add enough orange juice to measure 3 cups. In a bowl, whisk together pudding and orange juice until smooth, about 2 minutes.

Fold in yogurt and orange sections. Spoon evenly into six small cups, if desired. Chill until ready to serve.

Apple Crisp

Yes, it is possible (and easy) to create a home-baked dessert on the water. Serve the crisp warm with a prepared whipped topping or vanilla yogurt.

Serves 4 to 6
Prep time: 20 minutes
Baking time: 40 minutes

3 Golden Delicious apples
¼ cup granulated sugar
1 teaspoon fresh lemon juice
½ cup orange marmalade
10 whole cinnamon graham crackers (1 packet from
    a 3-packet, 1-pound box)
5 tablespoons unsalted butter, melted and cooled

Preheat oven to 350°F. Grease an 8½-inch round foil baking pan.

Peel, core, and thinly slice apples. In a large bowl, toss apples with sugar, lemon juice, and marmalade until mixed well. Spread evenly in prepared pan.

One packet of graham crackers yields 1¾ cups crumbs. Three apples yield 4 cups.

Place graham crackers in a gallon-size resealable bag. Using a rolling pin or heavy glass bottle, crush graham crackers into coarse crumbs. Pour butter into bag and knead to mix thoroughly. Spread crumb mixture evenly over apples.

Bake for 20 minutes. Lay a sheet of foil lightly over crumbs to prevent over-browning and bake for 20 minutes more, or until apples are tender. Serve hot, warm, or at room temperature.

VARIATIONS

Two 15- to 15¼-ounce cans of sliced peaches or pears, drained, may be used instead of the apples. Omit the sugar and reduce baking time to 20 minutes total.

Chopped nuts may be added to the crumb topping. Try walnuts for apples and pears and almonds for peaches.

Chocolate Marshmallow Crème Fudge

Makes 64 (1-inch) pieces
Prep time: 10 minutes plus chilling
Cooking time: 5 minutes

1 (7-ounce) jar marshmallow crème
1½ cups granulated sugar
1 (5½-ounce) can evaporated milk (⅔ cup)
¼ cup (½ stick) butter or margarine
½ teaspoon salt
1 (12-ounce) bag milk chocolate chips
1 (6-ounce) bag semi-sweet chocolate chips
2 teaspoons vanilla extract
⅓ cup chopped walnuts (optional)

Line an 8-inch square pan with foil.

In a large saucepan over medium heat, combine the marshmallow crème, sugar, evaporated milk, butter and salt. Bring to a full boil, stirring, and continue boiling for 5 minutes, stirring constantly.

Remove from heat and add the milk chocolate and semi-sweet chocolate chips. Stir until chocolate is melted and mixture is smooth. Stir in vanilla and walnuts. Pour into prepared pan. Chill for 2 hours, or until firm. Using the foil, lift fudge from the pan. Cut into 1-inch pieces. Store fudge in an airtight container at room temperature.

VARIATION

In place of the walnuts, stir in dried cranberries or cherries, toffee bits or Butterfinger bits, white chocolate chips, mini-marshmallows, or crushed Oreo cookies.

Whip up a batch of fudge after breakfast and surprise the crew at lunch. Or make it at home and pack in a tin lined with wax paper.

TIP

Fudge can also be made in two loaf pans (one for home, one to travel).

Chocolate Date-Nut Bars

This simple-to-make confection turns after-dinner coffee into an occasion. They're easy to transport, so you might want to make these bars before departure.

Makes about 40 pieces
Prep time: 10 minutes, plus chilling
Cooking time: 5 minutes

1 (12-ounce) bag semi-sweet chocolate chips
⅔ cup chopped pecans or walnuts
⅔ cup chopped dates
1 cup sweetened flaked coconut

Line an 11½ by 8-inch pan with waxed paper.

In a saucepan over very low heat, melt chocolate, stirring occasionally. Remove from heat. Fold in nuts and dates.

Spread mixture in prepared pan. Sprinkle coconut over top and lightly press into mixture with a clean spoon or spatula. Chill until firm. Cut into pieces.

TIP

Toast any extra coconut and sprinkle it on fruit or cereal for breakfast.

VARIATION
Use dried cherries or cranberries in place of the dates and any type of nuts that you prefer.

Easy Raspberry Trifle

Given the right combination, prepared ingredients can be transformed into an elegant dessert. See the tip on page 139 for an even more streamlined version that's ideal for making while you're on board.

Serves 6
Prep time: 25 minutes

2 (3 to 4 ounces each) packages commercially prepared
   lady fingers
½ cup seedless raspberry jam
¼ cup sherry, rum, spiced rum or apple juice
2 cups milk
1 package vanilla instant pudding mix
1 (8-ounce) container extra-creamy whipped topping, thawed
½ cup mini chocolate chips, or grated semi-sweet chocolate
Chocolate syrup for drizzling

Split lady fingers and spread one side of each with raspberry jam. Replace top halves to form sandwiches. Arrange half the lady fingers in bottom of a 2-quart glass soufflé dish or casserole. Sprinkle with sherry, rum, spiced rum or apple juice.

Prepare pudding by whisking milk into mix. Let stand for 3 minutes. Spoon half the pudding over the lady fingers.

Stir whipped topping and chocolate chips together and spread half the mixture over the pudding. Repeat layers. Cover tightly and refrigerate several hours or overnight.

To serve, drizzle the chocolate syrup decoratively over the trifle. Pass more chocolate syrup on the side.

The ingredients can be taken on board and put together a few hours ahead. For convenience, use four 4-ounce cups of prepared pudding in place of the pudding mix and milk.

T
I
P

Iced Mocha

Serves 4
Prep time: 5 minutes

4 cups whole or low-fat milk
4 teaspoons instant espresso powder
6 tablespoons chocolate syrup

In a large bowl, whisk the milk into the espresso powder until the powder is dissolved. Stir in chocolate syrup.

To serve chilled, place 3 ice cubes in each of 4 tall glasses and pour the mocha mixture over the ice. To serve hot, pour into a medium saucepan and heat over medium-low heat until mixture is just scalded.

A drink for all seasons—cool and refreshing in the summer and warm and comforting when colder weather comes around.

Cranberry Pink Lemonade

Serves 4
Prep time: 5 minutes

2 cups cranberry juice cocktail
1⅓ cups pink lemonade
⅔ cup orange juice
Lemon slices for garnish

In a large pitcher or bowl, stir together the cranberry juice, lemonade, and orange juice. Serve over ice in 4 tall glasses. Garnish with the lemon slices.

This refreshing take on lemonade will become a standard on your boat. It's a great drink for a kid's birthday party.

Guava Punch

For a nonalcoholic punch, omit the bitters in this recipe.

Serves 4
Prep time: 5 minutes

2 cups guava or papaya nectar
1 (12-ounce) can ginger ale
¼ cup fresh lime juice
¼ cup alcohol-free grenadine
1 tablespoon bitters (optional)

In a pitcher or large bowl, stir together nectar, ginger ale, lime juice, grenadine, and bitters. Serve over ice cubes in 4 tall glasses.

Rum Punch

Guava and pineapple juices are available in 12-ounce cans, which makes this punch a snap to mix on board. But if you prefer, you can make the punch mixture (with or without the rum) ahead.

Serves 4
Prep time: 5 minutes

1 (12-ounce) can guava juice
1 (12-ounce) can pineapple juice
1½ cups orange juice
1 cup light or dark rum
6 tablespoons grenadine
6 lime wedges
Freshly grated nutmeg for garnish

In a 2-quart container, combine guava, pineapple, and orange juices. Stir in rum and grenadine. Serve over ice cubes in tall glasses. Garnish each glass with a lime wedge and nutmeg.

To make individual portions, combine 2 ounces each of guava, pineapple, and orange juices. Stir in 1½ ounces of rum and 1 tablespoon grenadine.

VARIATIONS
There are a variety of tropical juices available…try them! A dash of grapefruit juice may be added to each drink. Additional rum, preferably dark, may be floated on top.

Easy Entertaining

Entertaining is part of the fun of boating. Whether it's a family birthday, a special holiday, or just an impromptu gathering of old or new friends at the harbor, there are easy ways to turn it into an occasion. Creating a festive atmosphere can be fun. Take advantage of being on the water—it provides a beautiful backdrop that doesn't need much dressing up. Enhance the setting with a few simple, easy-to-transport decorations such as balloons, festive swizzle sticks, and colorful napkins. They don't take up much space, and they add just the right touch at a variety of parties.

As you plan your party menu, give some thought to food presentation and bring along a few items to use as garnishes or to add color to dishes. Red cabbage leaves make a great liner for trays or salad bowls. Thin slices of lemon or orange can dress up drinks.

Remember that the cook is supposed to enjoy the party, too. Your guests will also understand the challenges of entertaining on the water and will not expect elaborate preparations. In fact, by keeping it simple, you'll keep the atmosphere relaxed and that translates into happy guests and hosts.

Child's Birthday Party

A birthday on the water turns the event into an adventure. Balloons, festive napkins, and streamers add to the atmosphere.

Taco Bake (page 88)
Carrot Salad (page 110)
Birthday cake
Cranberry Pink Lemonade (page 139)

HINTS

• Bake square cake layers of the child's favorite cake at home for easy packing and wrap well. You can make them a week ahead and freeze them. They can be stored in resealable plastic bags in a cooler until the party.

• Make a simple confectioners' sugar and butter icing and tint it with a little food coloring. (It can be made ahead and brought in a plastic container or made on board.) Ice and decorate the cake shortly before the party. Candies such as licorice strings, Life Savers, and sprinkles can be used for decorations. Don't forget the candles. The carrot salad can be made ahead.

• Dress up the lemonade by making fruit "stirrers" for each drink: Thread pineapple chunks, strawberries, grapes, or other fruits on wooden skewers.

French Picnic

Marinated Olives (page 64)
Shrimp Ahoy (page 63)
Potato Salad with Smoked Oysters (page 108)
Selection of cheeses
Breads or crackers
Grapes

HINTS

- Marinate the olives well in advance. The potato salad can be made ahead, as can the marinade for the shrimp.

- Serve the shrimp on skewers with cucumbers, as suggested in the recipe. A jar or plastic container with a hinged lid is great for serving the olives.

- If you have a picnic basket, bring it with you and fill it with napkins and utensils for lunch. You can use it to stow other items when it's not in use for the picnic.

Whether you go ashore or stay on board, this elegant, but lazy lunch is just right for a warm day.

Southern-Style Breakfast

Grits Cakes (page 94, sidebar)
Bacon
Melon wedges
Breads or crackers
Cinnamon Rolls (page 127) or purchased

HINTS

- The grits can be made and chilled ahead, as can the melon slices.

- For extra flavor, cook the bacon first, then cook the grits cakes in the same skillet in some of the bacon fat.

- You might also want to try the precooked bacon described on page 121.

Breakfasts in the South are hearty! Surprise the crew on a Sunday morning with a special feast. Use gingham napkins for atmosphere.

Anniversary Dinner for Two

Splurge for that special dinner. Bring some nice linen napkins from home and maybe even a single red rose. Little tea light candles will help set the mood.

Sun-dried Tomato Spread on toasts (page 58)
Grilled Beef Tenderloin with Horseradish Sauce (page 81)
Chilled Asparagus with Herb-Garlic Vinaigrette (page 47)
Herbed Potatoes (page 111)
Warm Sautéed Bananas (page 135)

HINTS

- Make the spread and the toasts ahead.

- Steam some fresh asparagus at home and bring them on board chilled. You can also make the dressing ahead. Drizzle the asparagus with the dressing about 30 minutes before serving.

- Buy a small tenderloin for this dinner. You'll still have leftovers for a salad or sandwiches the next day.

Cocktails at Sundown

Possibly the perfect type of party for a boat. After a day in the sun, it's nice to relax with a refreshing rum punch (or a non-alcoholic punch) and a few hors d'oeuvres.

Brie and Apricot Quesadillas (page 65)
Bean and Salsa Dip (page 61)
Veggies with Sesame-Tahini Sauce (page 60)
Spiced peanuts or almonds (purchased)
Rum Punch (page 140)

HINTS

- Add fresh fruit or even tiny paper umbrellas to the drinks for a festive touch.

- The sesame-tahini sauce and bean dip can be made ahead. As for veggies, they can be cut up in advance and kept chilled until party time. Bring along some toasted sesame seeds to sprinkle on top of the dip.

- The quesadilla recipe can be expanded or contracted, depending on the number of guests.

4th of July Barbecue

Barbecued Shrimp Kebabs (page 100)
Grilled Marinated Steak (page 46)
Coleslaw
Old-Fashioned Corn Bread (page 128)
Cherry-Chocolate Brownies (page 130)
Watermelon
Lemonade and iced tea

HINTS

- Make the barbecue sauce for the shrimp ahead.

- Taking a whole watermelon on board might be difficult. Either purchase the small round "Sugar Baby" variety or cut it yourself before you leave and pack it in a rigid plastic container.

- For the corn bread, stir about 1 cup of shredded cheddar cheese into the batter before baking.

- If you have a portable CD player, bring along some all-American tunes to play during the party.

Fly the flag and hang red, white and blue streamers for a patriotic celebration. Pull out all the stops and offer a "surf and turf" choice for the main course.

Sunday Brunch

Perfect on a lazy Sunday, this menu is easy on the cook.

Pasta Pancake (page 114)
Green or vegetable salad
Grilled Ham Steaks with Orange-Honey Glaze (page 123)
Citrus-Spiced Fruit (page 134)

HINTS

- Make the fruit ahead and bring it on board in a plastic container. Top it with a little vanilla yogurt dusted with some cinnamon or nutmeg.

- The salad can be pot luck. For example, you can drizzle leftover grilled or steamed vegetables with a vinaigrette dressing or combine a selection of chopped raw veggies with a dip that can be made ahead.

- Cook the pasta for the pancake ahead, then cook the pancake a little bit ahead, if you like. It's delicious at room temperature. Sprinkle it with chopped herbs or scallion tops for color.

Grown-Up Birthday Party

Warm Spinach and Feta Dip with Olives (page 62)
Beef Kebabs (page 82)
Grilled Vegetables (page 70)
Pound Cake (page 132)
Hot fudge sauce

HINTS

- Most of this menu can be prepared ahead. The dip can be mixed at home and heated when ready to serve. For dippers, use pita wedges and cherry tomatoes. Depending on the timing, you can either marinate the meat ahead or make the marinade ahead. The vegetables can also be cut ahead and marinated.

- If you have decorative metal skewers, this is the time to use them.

- Select a special wine just for this dinner and spice up the after-dinner coffee by sprinkling in a little cinnamon before brewing.

- The pound cake can, of course, also be made ahead. Heat the fudge sauce just before serving.

Balloons and streamers say "party" for an adult, too. For a grown-up touch, you might also want to bring flowers, if it's feasible, as well as festive napkins and a tablecloth.

Metric Conversion Chart

LENGTH

If you know:	Multiply by:	To find:
Inches	25.0	Millimeters
Inches	2.5	Centimeters
Feet	30.0	Centimeters
Yards	0.9	Meters
Miles	1.6	Kilometers
Millimeters	0.04	Inches
Centimeters	0.4	Inches
Meters	3.3	Feet
Meters	1.1	Yards
Kilometers	0.6	Miles

VOLUME

If you know:	Multiply by:	To find:
Teaspoons	5.0	Milliliters
Tablespoons	15.0	Milliliters
Fluid ounces	30.0	Milliliters
Cups	0.24	Liters
Pints	0.47	Liters
Quarts	0.95	Liters
Gallons	3.8	Liters
Milliliters	0.03	Fluid ounces
Liters	4.2	Cups
Liters	2.1	Pints
Liters	1.06	Quarts
Liters	0.26	Gallons

WEIGHT

If you know:	Multiply by:	To find:
Ounces	28.0	Grams
Pounds	0.45	Kilograms
Grams	0.035	Ounces
Kilograms	2.2	Pounds

TEMPERATURE

If you know:	Multiply by:	To find:
Degrees Fahrenheit	0.56 (after subtracting 32)	Degrees Celsius
Degrees Celsius	1.8 (then add 8)	Degrees Fahrenheit

INDEX